CAREER CONFINEMENT

Eb—
Here's to helping
people [run free]
play in the
abundance!
♡ LIVE!

E P

Elvis

ELIZABETH PEARSON

CAREER

CONFINEMENT

**HOW TO FREE YOURSELF,
FIND YOUR GUIDES,** and
SEIZE THE FIRE OF INSPIRED WORK

LIONCREST
PUBLISHING

CAREER CONFINEMENT

How to Free Yourself, Find Your Guides, and Seize the Fire of Inspired Work

FIRST EDITION

ISBN   978-1-5445-3403-9 *Hardcover*
       978-1-5445-3404-6 *Paperback*
       978-1-5445-3405-3 *Ebook*

For Delilah and Vivian. You've saved me in more ways than you'll ever know.

You are tigers. Stay fearless.

For Ryan. Thank you for not letting me retreat to the cage and proudly watching me run free.

For my clients. You have no idea how I've cherished being a part of your expansion.

Words can't express how insanely proud of you I am.

CONTENTS

INTRODUCTION

My intro is: there is no intro.

You don't have time to read an intro.

SEEING THE CAGE

Mohini was a beautiful, rare white tiger who was captured and confined in a popular zoo. She was the most popular attraction at the zoo, and people would travel from all over the country to see her.

Every person who came to see Mohini had the same reaction: initial awe followed by heartbreaking despair. This majestic animal was being kept in the old lion house, which was a twelve-by-twelve-foot cage. Each day, Mohini would pace back and forth...

back and forth...

back and forth...

As Mohini drew more and more attention, staff and biologists worked together to create a habitat that would mimic the beauty of her original home. It was several acres with hills, trees, flowers, and a pond. It was everything a tiger could want.

When they released Mohini into her new habitat, they realized they were too late.

Mohini was so accustomed to her cage that she wouldn't explore. She quickly scurried into a corner and refused to take a single step into the new space. She was blind to the beauty and freedom on the other side of her learned helplessness and fear of the unknown.

The staff tried and waited and watched for days, but Mohini stayed in her corner, pacing back and forth, back and forth.

Years later, she died in that corner, leaving behind a worn patch of grass twelve feet wide.

Mohini (a real tiger) is like so many women today. We have had bars of external conditioning and internal judgment erected around us, one by one, until we have learned to live in our own cage. Some days we pace back and forth with more frenetic energy, but we stay in the cage where we think we can survive.

Every once in a while, we may see a glimpse of the beautiful habitat that's right there. We glimpse the dream we had as a child. We see someone living an incredible life and wonder with jealousy why *we* can't have that.

Your habitat is for you alone, but you'll never get to experience all of the wonderful, fulfilling parts of it until you are brave enough to take a step out of your cage.

When women come to me, they are all in different cages: a failing relationship, a self-loathing mindset, a profession that no longer serves their Soul, or they've fallen prey to patriarchal external conditioning. They are scared to step out beyond the bars into their full power. I understand—the cage can feel secure and safe. But, if you sit still and reach deep into yourself, you'll feel a restlessness. That is your Soul begging you to go play in the unlimited abundance that's just on the other side of your fear.

It's time for you to see your cage for what it is. You may feel like your bars are very thin and widely spaced. You may feel like your bars are solid walls you can't even see through. No matter where you are in your journey, this book will help you break free and go play in your habitat that's just waiting for you to take your first step into the grass.

STEPPING OUT OF MY CAGE

"What are we going to *do* with you?"

I was both relieved and terrified to hear these words come out of my boss's mouth. I was too expensive for the startup skin-care company I'd been leading US sales for, and the more grueling travel I did and decks I built, the more unfulfilled I'd become. Monthly flights from SoCal to Halifax, Nova Scotia, or Rhode Island were completely draining me. My anxiety was sky-high and I was starting to feel like a caged animal. At the time, the care of our daughters, Delilah, five, and Vivian, two, was 100 percent on my and my husband's shoulders, as we had no support system in California. All of our friends and family (aka *free* babysitters) were in Illinois. Every time I left for a buyer meeting, my heart sank and a wave of panic and anxiety would wash over me—from the moment my car backed out of the driveway to go to the airport until the moment I got my arms around them when I got home.

There was one night in particular when I was tucking in Delilah and telling her, while choking back tears, that I would once again be gone on a work trip by the time she woke. She could see the pain in my eyes—the mom guilt taking hold. Then out of her little five-year-old mouth she said, "Why do you have to go if you don't want to go?"

I replied, "I have to go because it's my job and I have to make money."

Delilah: "But you say that we can do anything we want when we grow up."

"Yes, you're right. That's true."

Delilah: "So why can't you do whatever you want to do?"

Damn. She was right. Nothing like a child to throw your "words of wisdom" back in your face to force an Oprah-level aha moment. I was telling my girls one thing and doing another. I was modeling hypocrisy rather than how to be strong enough to believe that I deserved to be deeply happy, not only at home, but in my career. After that night, there was no going back. My hand was forced because as I allowed myself to wither away, I was being watched…closely.

The next day I told my boss, "I'm just going to go." I could hear the relief in her voice. We both knew it was for the best. I proceeded to negotiate a generous severance, and to this day, I maintain a close relationship with my ex-boss, the founder and CEO of Skinfix.

After I left my lucrative sales career, I decided it was time to start my own company. I was one of those people always spouting,

"Someday I'm just gonna do my own thing. Not sure what it is yet, but making old white guys richer sure as shit isn't my 'Purpose.'"

I had about a two-week grace period where I felt great. I spent that time perusing the aisles at Target, getting to know my Starbucks baristas, and smothering my kids. But after the newness wore off, I was hit by tidal waves of self-doubt and resistance, months and months of them. I call this the "Oh Fuck" period. I cried constantly. I felt lost, as if my personal value was dependent on my professional ability to earn. My whole identity had been tied to my career—now that that was gone, what did I have? I knew deep in my heart that I wanted to be my own boss—but I was terrified of both starting the process and not making money.

I had no idea what the "it" was that I was meant to, or even could, do. Convinced the time wasn't right, I sought refuge in my old not-so-comfortable comfort zone (aka the cage). My new plan was to start interviewing with a handful of companies that sold brands I loved and connected with.

I made it to third- and fourth-round interviews with three companies, flying to and from San Francisco and Minneapolis, but in the end, the offers I was expecting didn't come or were lowballs. Little did I understand at the time, but my Soul was whispering to me that none of those jobs would be worth sacrificing my dream of being my own boss. She (my Soul) knew I didn't really *want* any of those jobs—and there's no doubt that the hiring managers could feel that.

In the end, none of them felt exciting, so either they walked away from me or I walked away from them.

I know now that the Universe was refusing to let me take a job that wasn't in alignment with my Soul, but at the time, it rocked my self-confidence. I thought, *Oh my God, I'm fucked. I'm never going to get another job, at least not one that pays me what I'm worth.*

I also had a gnawing thought: *how many times am I going to ignore these messages and signs that the Universe is trying to get me to see?* My gut knew the time was now or never. If I had caved to the pressure to go get just *any* job—I wouldn't have been able to get one equal to or better than my previous one—it would have been Soul crushing. I couldn't let myself, or my daughters, down like that. Instead, I needed to figure it the fuck out. It was time to stop talking about "doing my own thing" and start doing it.

Those beginning months of uncertainty were brutal. I dove into the deep end of creating a website (I'm talking ten-hour days creating it and learning how to code), lots of working out (distraction), lots of consuming podcasts, and "studying up" on how to be an entrepreneur from people like Gary Vee, Lewis Howes, Jesse Itzler, and Jack Canfield (notice how there were zero female "mentors"?).

There were days when I cried intermittently and commiserated with former colleagues. I felt completely alone, yet at the same time responsible for "making it" and showing family and friends that it could be done.

On one particularly low day, Ryan was traveling for work and I was driving my daughters to school and white-knuckling it. My thoughts screaming, *Keep it together, bitch!* I'd been crying for weeks. I was desperate to know I was going to be okay. A few days before, I had finished reading a book about how to ask questions to the Universe and decode the responses. The idea was that the Universe was always listening (and I was *desperate* to know that someone was hearing my call for help). The book was *E-Squared* by author Pam Grout, who talked about asking the Universe or our Angel Squad for a gift, such as to see a penny or something small. I thought, *Screw that, I need a big sign. I don't need a gift. I don't want a flat-screen TV or a good parking spot at Costco. I need a sign that my life didn't just fucking implode.*

While in the car, I silently asked my angels to show me an orange bus. And as my Jeep groaned up the steep Southern California hill and crested at the top, I saw eight orange school buses, which may not seem out of the ordinary to you, but here's the thing: our district does not have school buses—like any.

Every single day I dropped my kids off at school, there had never once been a single orange bus. But on this day, at the top of this hill, there were eight. A skeptic, I immediately amended my request and said, out loud, "It can't be a *school* bus." From the back seat, my girls looked at me like I'd gone mad, because I was both talking to myself and crying. I thought, *There! I'll show you. You're going to have to earn my belief. I'm no sucker.*

After coming home from drop-off, I picked back up where I left off, which was to swing from frantically working on my business plan to bouts of crying. To break this cycle, I told myself I needed to get some fresh air in the sun, and went for a run through my neighborhood. I ran up our biggest hill, feeling empty and spent. Without energy to go forward, I paused at the top of the hill. And as I raised my head, I was dumbfounded.

Sure as shit, an impeccably maintained, high-shine, orangest of orange 1963 Volkswagen Bus was coming up the hill right at me. It was driven by a guy with giant sunglasses, a brown beard, and a huge smile on his face. As he got closer, and my jaw dropped, he slid down his sunglasses, looked into my eyes—and what felt like into the depth of my tattered Soul—extended his arm out the window, and flashed me the peace sign before gradually driving off into the horizon.

I burst into tears, threw my hands up to the sky, and thanked the Universe for showing me a sign my rational brain could not dismiss. This was it. I had asked if it was all going to be okay, which is all any of us ever want to feel, and the Universe was telling me, loud and clear, that the lane to "do my own thing" was wide open. All I had to do was get behind the wheel, even if I didn't know how to get where I wanted to go. The "cage" had never been locked.

That moment when I was forced to believe, without the shadow of a doubt, that I was not on this journey alone, is burned into my brain. Now, when I feel scared, lost, or alone, I remember that moment, and the trust and emotion that I experienced.

I want you to have that same moment. That bone-deep certainty that this is a path we travel together. However alone you've felt before, it all changes now.

THIS BOOK *IS* FOR YOU

If you feel alone...

If you feel unvalued...

If you feel stuck…

If you feel like you're off Purpose…

If you're reading this, odds are you're incredibly high functioning, but you're likely going about achieving results the hard way: the way you've been taught, rather than the way our divine 75-percent-nonphysical-portion of us wants us to. We don't have to work so damn hard. The first step is to see ourselves as the divine perfection we already are and then throw out the playbook (which was male created BTW) that says we need to over sacrifice, grind, and hustle our way to "success"—which is often a destination that leaves us feeling empty.

Instead, we need to rely on this massive untapped asset—the guidance we are constantly receiving from our Spiritual Board of Advisors, which includes our Soul, guides, and ancestors. They are constantly pointing us to total alignment with our jobs, family, and everything external.

Before we continue on though, take a moment to give yourself some grace and gentleness. No "transformation" needs to happen.

You are whole and perfect as you are, right now, in this moment.

You have goals and desires, but achievement of those will not increase your inherent, divine self-worth. I believe we want those things because we want to enjoy the *experience* of having them. We want to feel financial freedom so we can have the experience of travel, spoiling our loved ones, or pampering ourselves. And that's okay. It's better than okay, in fact: experiences are the reason we manifested into these meat-suits and are walking around in this dimension.

The path to getting all of those wonderful things though requires some guts and betting on yourself. It's damned near impossible to bet on yourself when your self-confidence isn't sky high. Over the years, it's been chipped away by external conditioning and one too many asshole bosses or partners. It's as if you're looking into a foggy mirror.

When the fog is there, you can't see your beautiful, genius, majestic self—the tiger you are. Which brings us to why you picked up, or were gifted, this book. I will give you tactics to wipe away the fog from the mirror to see clearly that you are a divine being and a powerful creator. We need to break through the lies and realize that even when the mirror is fogged, the reflection behind it is perfect, whether you can see it or not.

Can you guess the fastest way to **not** get what you want?

By beating yourself up. That's why you'll notice throughout these chapters that we don't do any "tearing you down to build you back up" bullshit. Fuck that. My goal with this book is to give you a hug. Yes, a big fat, squeezing-you-a-bit-too-hard and holding-on-a-bit-too-long hug. We're going to take that part of you that's been sitting in the corner, scrutinized and judged, and give that beautiful bitch a long hug. And we're not going to let go until that part of you succumbs to the hug, because you need it. There are so many voices out there, pointing fingers and yelling to try to "motivate" you, and most of those voices are yours. If all you take away from this book is to give yourself a break and not judge yourself, then every moment I spent on this book will have been worth it.

This book is going to urge you to be gentle with yourself—the opposite of what the patriarchy and every grind-it-out, entrepreneur, how-to book teaches. We need to dismiss that path because it was not made for us. That antiquated, patriarchal path doesn't take into consideration the magic we have as women. We are tuned in to our Spirits, operating on a level that can pick up energy frequencies. That is our GPS—it's the divine shortcut that we've been denying every time we try to compete solely using physical assets and abilities. Ladies, our new goal is to soar above the traditional path to success and be Soul-driven to heights that we can't even imagine.

WHAT YOU'LL LEARN

The goal of this book is to give you the tactics you need to see yourself and create your own unique path. By the end, you will:

- Make big changes quickly (because there's no time to waste).
- Set boundaries with friends and family (get ready to check some peeps).
- Connect to a deeper level of self-awareness (it's about to get real quiet up in here).
- Create an open dialogue with the nonphysical part of yourself (give the inner you the mic).
- Learn to take directions from Soul GPS (it's your superpower and unfair advantage to getting everything you want in your career).

In order to keep this book to an unscary length, I've pared down on some of the activities. If you want more information on any of the guidance in this book or if you prefer to have a worksheet to start from, download my app: EP Coaching. It has a whole section dedicated to worksheets and additional information that supports the teachings in this book.

FOLLOWING THE PATH

Each chapter of this book will tell you the story of a client, with names and some specifics changed to protect their privacy. Their stories are from my perspective as their coach and my only intention in sharing them is that you the reader can see that no matter what situation they were in, they've always been tigers—even if they couldn't see it for themselves. The common thread is that they were all facing some type of resistance and (most) overcame it using specific tactics and allowing our journey together to be Soul led. Look for similarities in their stories. Which ones can you see yourself in?

You'll also hear stories of times I was knee deep in the shit but was pulled forward by the relentless trust that there was a greater force who had a plan, and my only job was to decode the clues for the answers and next steps.

Then, you'll hear from our Guiding Light, a spiritual expert who will help us understand the chapter's lesson. Each GL is someone who has either been a "coach in my head," a guest on my podcast, or a lifebuoy that was divinely thrown my way when I felt I was drowning. Their insights not only helped me break out of my Career Confinement but have been the secret weapons to jumpstarting hundreds of my clients' successful escapes.

Finally, you'll explore the lesson for yourself, putting the tactics provided into action. While every chapter is applicable to everyone, they each focus on a specific type of person, so if you're short on time, skip straight to the one you need the most.

Chapter Two: I Think I Lost You

Why you've lost connection to your inner GPS and how to fix it. This chapter is for the ones trying to play by the patriarchy's playbook.

Chapter Three: Screw "How?"

Why trusting your angel horde is your only job. This chapter is for all the dreamers who doubt.

Chapter Four: It's an Inside Job

Material things will never truly bring you happiness. This chapter is for all the workaholics.

Chapter Five: The Real F-Bomb

Why fear is causing you to play small and how to break free. This chapter is for all the young millennials.

Interlude: The Big Move

Chapter Six: Let Go or Be Dragged

Why "bad" things happen when you resist expansion and growth. This chapter is for all the skeptics.

Chapter Seven: Yeah, But

Excuses and blame limit your power and tempt you to succumb to mediocrity. This chapter is for the ones who are hiding behind their kids.

Chapter Eight: Move the Moped

You can't get the Range Rover until you move the moped. This chapter is for anyone who knows they're settling.

Interlude: Devil on My Shoulder

Chapter Nine: Productivity Does Not Equal Worth

Get more by doing less. This chapter is for all the high-functioning overachievers.

Chapter Ten: Believe It to See It

You can be a manifest creator, if only you believe in yourself. This chapter is for those who think they suck at meditation.

Chapter Eleven: Gratitude Is a Verb

An attitude of gratitude can get you everything you want or keep you stuck. This chapter is for those who feel they're being prematurely pushed out to pasture.

Interlude: A Lesson in Humility

Chapter Twelve: Forgive Yourself

Taking the megaphone away from your inner critic can be life changing. This chapter is for those living with shame.

Chapter Thirteen: Burn the Boats

You can escape from the mundane, but you have to have the courage to burn the boats. This chapter is for those who know, deep down, they're meant for epic shit.

WHY TRUST ME?

This is where I need you to have a bit of faith. I know "coaches" are a dime a dozen and there are a million other business and self-help books out there—most with a truck ton of comforting Amazon reviews. So why spend your precious and valuable time reading this book?

Because not long ago, I too was living in confinement, and that shit is still fresh. I struggled for years to prove myself to bosses and jobs that didn't value me, selling products that I no longer loved. I spent over a decade reading self-help books and going on retreats, begging for guidance that would calm and lead both my professional and spiritual sides. Yet everything I found made me choose one bucket: spirit *or* business. But are they not completely dependent on each other's fulfillment?

I wanted to write the book I needed—for women who are successful but are undervalued, overworked, and at odds with their true Purpose. I've helped hundreds of women get unstuck and achieve their highest goals in their personal and professional lives, and make a lot of money as a result. And if you're holding this book, now it's your turn. If your mom, your girlfriend, or your boss gave it to you, or forced it upon you, it's because they love you and are tired of waiting for you to see the genius, untethered, goddess version of yourself that they see.

I want to make this clear: I'm not claiming to be an "expert." There's no spirituality degree I can hold up and say, "I know it all." I am merely a seeker who's read a ton of books, done a bunch of homework, applied what I learned, and gave the CliffsNotes to other women to help them break free from the cage of mediocrity. I am well aware that there are no new ideas and that's why you'll see every nugget of wisdom cited and credited to the Guiding Light that I learned it from.

Have you ever heard of a chef who was self-taught and became exceptionally good at it? That's how I approached my spiritual education. Desperation can birth incredible feats including becoming a subject matter expert—and I was desperate. I was in pain for many years, and I knew that if I wanted to stay on the physical plane, I needed hope. I needed to learn how to be comfortable on this earth and find joy during my time here. One of my favorite authors, Rebecca Campbell, beautifully explains, "We all have an inner light waiting to guide us home. But sometimes the Universe turns off all the lights, so we have no choice but to find our own."

To find the comfort of my own light, I started reading and learning from what I've dubbed Guiding Lights—you'll meet them in this book. It didn't take long for it to turn into an obsession, and it eventually led to my coaching business.

I have two intentions for this book:

1. Print exactly two copies and place them in each of my daughters' hands so when they grow into women, they can see that they too can do hard things.
2. Be the friend, supporter, and cheerleader you need to see that you are a fucking tiger and **you deserve it all**.

WHAT TO EXPECT FROM THIS BOOK

It's my opinion that self-help "experts" don't know shit about what's right for you. They only know what's right for *them*. You're the only one who knows what's best for you. Thought leaders and Guiding Lights are merely trying to help you see that. They know they don't have the answers, but their hope is that their words will help jump-start you to hear the answers living inside you. And if you want to learn how to hear and receive your Soul's GPS guidance, this book can help get you there.

This book is not a lecture or a sermon.

It's not a judgment of where you are right now.

I'm not telling you what to do, rather offering options.

It is a guidebook full of great tactics that can help you, but you don't *have* to do any of it. I want to help you listen to *yourself* because your Soul already knows what to do.

If you get to the end and this book doesn't resonate with you, that's okay. You may not be ready yet. That's not a judgment of who you are, where you are, or how you got there. It just means that now's not the right time.

This book isn't going anywhere. It will be like a warm blanket waiting for you on the couch. When you're ready to snuggle up, that's when your emancipation from confinement will begin.

This book is not a loophole for you to do nothing and then get pissed when nothing happens. While it's full of tactics that can help you get the information you want in a quick and concise way, you can't skip the journey.

You have to do the work. It's as if there's a dark and scary forest lying ahead. You have no idea what's in it, but we're going to walk through it together, my hand gently on your back guiding you to paths that I've taken clients down before. You're going to have to take the steps forward, but you're going to reach the other side less bruised and battered—and much faster—than if you were to go it alone. My hand on your back will also ensure that you don't turn around and go back to your comfort zone cage.

You'll never be able to un-know what you read in this book, which ensures you'll never go back to being totally confined. You'll realize that the door to the cage isn't locked. You can walk the fuck out whenever you're ready to play in the magic that's on the other side of those bars (which are really just FEAR: False Evidence Appearing Real). And besides, the journey *is* the fun part, right? Everyone just wants to hurry up and manifest, but understanding your power as a creator *is* the manifestation. It won't work without belief.

As you read through this book, I encourage you to keep in mind this question: what's the downside?

What's the harm in believing in yourself?

What's the harm in staying open-minded to all sorts of magic and woo-woo?

To remind you, I'll end each chapter with a "what's the harm" question. After all, there's nothing to be lost by trying out these tactics—only things to be gained. The critical piece is that you stay open on this journey.

This journey starts by learning how to see through the fog.

I THINK I LOST YOU

HOW TO RECONNECT WITH YOUR INNER GPS

"I'm in the 'spiritual closet.' In tech, I feel like I have to be competitive and fight for everything I want. I'm scared of never having enough… and never being enough."

—SARA

MEET SARA

Sara is a single mother of two who was living in San Jose, working at a large software company, when we met. She came to me as a referral from another client, who told me, "Sara is so smart and bright. She has this incredible energy, but her company just isn't seeing it anymore." Sara was continually passed over for promotions, with no explanation as to why.

Now, Sara is the epitome of a bohemian beauty. She has gorgeous, long, flowing hair that's likely never seen a heat tool and yet still manages to look like Giselle's. She has beautiful dream catchers on the wall behind her, in full view during Zoom calls. She was not who you would think of as a "tech" woman. I was immediately intrigued on our initial call. My first thought was, "Is she in the right profession?"

Five minutes into the conversation, I knew she was. She was uber-polished and 100 percent professional tech. She had created double-digit growth for her company quarter after quarter. She was crushing it as one of their highest performers, yet the company kept promoting men over her. I knew the reason why as soon as I saw her: she didn't fit the mold. Because she didn't look or act the part, they kept promoting people who were less competent than her.

By the time she started working with me, Sara had put up with being overlooked for years, the last two of which she'd been very unhappy. The straw that broke the camel's proverbial back was when one of the men who worked *for* her was promoted *above* her.

As we started to work together, I dug into how she had lost her way. Why didn't she quit the first time she was passed over? It turned out to be directly tied to her home life.

Sara had two beautiful daughters, aged six and nine at the time, and she had recently gotten divorced from her husband of eighteen years. Her marriage was as unique as she was—they loved each other very much, but they wanted the freedom to explore and love others at the same time (very enlightened and boho, I thought).

Her husband dated a string of women during the open part of their marriage, and Sara spent five years dating an older man (before it eventually fizzled out). He was distinguished and professional on all levels. He showed her a new reality—what her life could be, one that she hadn't seen before. No surprise this made her husband feel very insecure, contributing even more to the downfall of their marriage.

She had started to let go of her self-worth and self-identity years before her difficulties at work. My hunch was that Sara had been settling for things that were well below what she deserved for some time.

This happens to so many women. Your Soul is telling you to seek out the best things in life—the best possible experiences—that are specifically for you. But when you start to ignore the Soul's GPS, which is trying to direct you toward your best self, you start to settle, both at home and at work.

Sara was unhappy at work because she was operating at a lower vibration in her day-to-day life. She was radiating out, "I'll take whatever you'll give me," because that's what was happening at home. Sara wanted to focus solely on her career during our sessions at first. She wasn't proactively talking about her marriage or the man she was currently dating (who was keeping her at arm's length because he didn't want to commit). However, she needed to work on her personal life in order to improve her professional life.

GUIDING LIGHT: ECKHART TOLLE

"Whenever you become anxious or stressed, outer purpose has taken over, and you've lost sight of your inner purpose. You have forgotten that your state of consciousness is primary, all else secondary."

—ECKHART TOLLE

Reconnection to your guidance system can only happen when you are rooted in the present moment, instead of planning for the future or living in the past. To be in spiritual alignment and hear the direction your Soul is giving you, you must be present, which means feeling the things around you: your emotions, your body, the ground under your feet. The essence of Eckhart is the realization that when you are in the present moment, you are in alignment with your Soul, and everything is fine.

Often when we're suffering or when we lose touch with our Soul's GPS, it's because we're either worried about the future or we're trying to understand and accept the past. Any time that you're transported mentally away from this moment, sitting in front of a computer or with this book in your hands, you are inviting suffering because we have no control over either past or future.

Eckhart tells us that being in the present moment while something undesirable is happening enables you to be present, regardless of your situation. For instance, you get a flat tire in the middle of the night. Don't resist the negativity. Stress comes from resisting the present moment. You don't have to embrace the pain, but you do have to accept it and know that it will eventually pass. You can choose to wallow in the pain and irritation, or you can accept the present moment as it is and be in a place of peace.

When we start to get upset about things in the past or the future, we're pulled out of that present moment. I get it. Being present is really hard to do, especially now when it feels like there are a million things we're constantly worrying about. However, it's just like anything else you do in life: the more you practice and work on it, the better you get at it.

Suffering is being in the past or the future. The most painful experience most women have is giving birth. I know for me it was extremely painful. But in that moment, even with the pain, I knew everything was okay. Even when we're in immense pain or feeling immense sadness, we need to take a beat, find our breath, and sit in that feeling. You'll realize that what you're feeling is manageable, it isn't killing you, and it's not nearly as bad as the suffering your mind can put you through by trying to live in the future or change the past.

In Sara's case, she needed to sit with her feelings in the present moment and decide that where she was no longer meeting the standards she had for her life. Understanding the root of her dissatisfaction gave her the courage to walk away. She accepted the bed she had made for herself and then committed to changing it. She knew she'd outgrown her "old life," and it was time to embrace uncertainty, trusting herself and the Universe to catch her on the other side if she took the leap—which it did.

OUT OF TOUCH

As we age, it becomes harder to stay in the present moment. We have more options, more distractions, and more responsibilities. But when we were younger, for example at age twenty-two, our Soul screamed the loudest about what it wanted out of life. When you're little, you're totally present so you may not know what you want to do, other than have a job that's fun. Then, when you're in your early twenties, you start to live more for the future and begin to create a vision for what you want out of your professional and personal life.

At twenty-two, I had just graduated college, and I knew exactly what I was going to do. My plan had always been to do some epic shit—not sell out and work for "the man" in corporate America. I wanted to rock the world. Be a disruptor. Blow some proverbial shit up. Be a changemaker. Be loud and have my voice heard.

I wanted to be free and untethered. To answer to no one (and make a ton of money doing it). And at twenty-two, I could run in any direction—I was a tiger running free. However, over time I started to believe the external conditioning: that I needed to follow the "rules" of a career playbook that was designed for men, by men. I bought into the cage that was slowly being erected around me and my big dreams. When that happened, I started to settle and conform. I let that voice be silenced so I could…get the house, get the title, be skinny at all costs, and fit in.

I accepted little consolation prizes instead of continually striving for my big vision. Sara did the same thing. Her dream was to own a tech company. While she was (kind of) doing the steps to get there, she had gotten stuck in the mud with the conditions of her last seven years, including her marriage and being overlooked at work. However, her twenty-two-year-old self would have called bullshit on that a long time ago.

Her mirror was getting foggy.

Let's chew on this concept a bit more. When we're young, we have a pretty clear picture of who we are and what we want to do. We may not know the specifics, but we do know the big values. We want to have a job that pays well so we can have freedom. We want to find a loving partner who appreciates us. We want to travel around the world. Twenty-two is the time of big daydreams. Crystal clear, grandiose visions that we can see like a freshly cleaned mirror. However, as we actually start to walk that path, little by little, the mirror begins to get a little foggy.

We default into some basic career just to get a job out of college because our parents are putting pressure on us to prove our worth. They want the return on the investment that they made in you over the last two decades. They want to brag to their friends that you are a so-and-so. You get the distinct feeling that it's time to put up or shut up. You end up taking the first job you can get to pay the bills and start paying back your student loans. Then, before you know it, five years go by. You justify it because you have to stay at your job at least a couple of years for it to count on your résumé, right?

After those five years, it feels like you've started to build experience. Why take the risk of switching career paths, even if it's going to put you on a path to the things your twenty-two-year-old self wanted? At not even thirty years old, we're already starting to lose touch. Up goes a bar to the cage.

Five more years and another job—one that pays even more. Now the mirror is getting really foggy thanks to the money and the false sense of security that cash is giving us. We put up with this path for a few more years. Up go a few more bars to the cage.

Then we have children, we start being martyrs, and the mirror is completely fogged. We're in our forties, and we don't see ourselves at all. We've completely lost touch. We don't see the Soul that was so excited to start this journey. All we can see is the fog of responsibilities, obligations, and laundry list of "shoulds." Now we're in a full-fledged cage.

But every now and then it happens. Somebody takes a finger to the mirror and wipes away one tiny piece of fog. That's the Spirit getting through, saying, "It's okay, I'm still here. I trust you. I still believe in us." Over time, if you let the Soul keep gently smudging away little pieces of fog from the mirror, you'll begin to see yourself again.

The objective of this book is to take the towel and completely wipe the mirror clean. When we wipe away that fog, we're wiping away:

- The lie that money and productivity equals our self-worth.
- The expectations that our partner has for us.
- The pressure to be something that your parents can proudly tell their friends you are.
- The vision of being a perfect mother, auntie, or friend.
- The compulsion to brag about how much money you make.

We're putting ourselves back into the driver's seat (by living in the present, as Eckhart would say). Once we unfog the mirror, we can understand that the only thing we need to worry about is what our Soul wants.

SPIRITUAL STEPS

Sara needed to be still. She needed to stop everything to take stock of all of the sacrifices she made to get to where she was. She had taken a big, risky leap moving to tech and thrived almost immediately—becoming a top performer in a heavily male-dominated space. She needed to clear her foggy mirror to see herself and the reality of her accomplishments.

To start, we needed to get clear on the current plan, so we did a Life Visioning exercise. The point is to clearly define your ideal day by asking a series of questions, such as:

- What time do you wake up?
- Are you working out first thing?
- Do you have time to sit and have coffee by yourself before you get your children ready?
- What time do you start work?
- Is it remote?
- What city are you in?
- What do you see when you look outside?
- What's the weather like?

By understanding your typical day, you can start down the path to what you want your future to be. However, while it's good to have vision and clarity about what you want, don't fall into the trap of living for that hope. "I'll be happy when…" Banish that thought. Be happy *now*. Be in this perfect present moment. Feeling grateful for your current situation will create space for your future desires to manifest.

Sound counterintuitive? It's not. What I mean is to be present in the moment and ground yourself in your current environment while you think about the future. Then you can use those thoughts to take action in the present.

I also had Sara map out three long-term and three short-term goals. Write down what you want in the next six months to a year (short-term) and then what you want in the next three to five years (long-term).

Most people have loose goals such as, "I want a nicer car. I want to have financial freedom." But you need to be *super* specific. It's like the Universe is a barista at Starbucks. If you walked in and said, "I'd like one coffee," they'd immediately have follow-up questions that would force you to get specific before they could fulfill your order. The Universe is the exact same.

Instead of saying I'd like a new car, you must decide the make, model, year, exterior color, interior color, etc. Be sure to think about WHY you want that new car. Is it to feel cozy and comfy on your drive to work? Is it to flex to your neighbors or make your parents proud? Really examine the "why" behind all the experiences you want to manifest.

Most of the time you want certain things because of how you think you'll feel when you get them. For example, you want more money because you think money will help you feel safe. But in this present moment, are you not safe? Most likely you are, so what do you really need the money for? Maybe the answer is to help your family feel financially secure. That's a positive intention—helping others—versus having money to buy designer labels in order to be liked or feel superior to others. Knowing your WHY will help you decide if you really want something and clarify the importance of wanting it.

Next, you have to write down what you want. Many clients want to skip this step and assume that just thinking about the "stuff" and visualizing having it will be enough, but it speeds up manifestation when you take pen to paper.

After you've written down the goal, add in great detail how you'll feel when you achieve the goal. The more you focus on the feeling, the easier it is to get excited about your goal and to associate it with positive emotions.

Take action to support the manifestation of those goals. For instance, say you want to live in another city within a year. You would start by setting up Zillow alerts within your budget to understand the market and see the available options. Then, look at the cost of living for that city. Once you know your housing and cost of living budgets, you can back-into what your salary needs to be.

The final step is crucial: release your attachment to how or when your goals manifest.

Download my app, EP Coaching, to get a Life Visioning worksheet.

Short-term, Sara wanted to get the hell out of her current job. She knew she had to leave; there was no salvaging it (or as I like to say, there was no more meat on the bone). Long-term, Sara wanted to start her own tech company. However, that's such a broad goal, it was hard to take a step toward it, so we broke it into smaller, actionable short-term goals.

The Universe wants to bless you. Sara had a wonderful, spiritual head start because she was open. That's all you need to be. She changed her perception of what she deserved, and when she made the decision to leave her job no matter what, the Universe rewarded her. Making the decision is the catalyst that ensures alignment with the next opportunity.

PROFESSIONAL STEPS

The first step Sara took was to rework her LinkedIn. Sara's mirror was so foggy that she no longer had an awareness of how good she was at her job. Like many of my clients, she had huge resistance around updating her résumé and her LinkedIn. On the surface, it sounds like a pain-in-the-ass thing to do, and I know that LinkedIn is not a "fun" social media platform. However, once I dig a little deeper with my clients, they realize that their resistance is really because they are trying to hide.

The most popular line from *Dirty Dancing* is, "Nobody puts baby in the corner." Sara, like most women, put herself in the corner by refusing to have high visibility or claiming credit for the achievements she made.

Sara had to start from the ground up on her LinkedIn. She didn't even have a banner, one of the basic elements that tells the algorithm that you have an active account, which in turn increases your SEO and your chances of being seen by a recruiter. When I pushed Sara on why she didn't want to list her accomplishments, she said a common refrain, "I didn't do it by myself. I was part of a team." Men never say this. They have no problem taking credit for a project's success. Women, however, hesitate to claim their achievements on their résumé or LinkedIn.

But LinkedIn is your website. Recruiters, hiring managers, key colleagues, and networking opportunities are always going to google you. When they do, the first thing that will show in the results is your LinkedIn, usually followed by your Instagram and Facebook. If your LinkedIn looks ignored or outdated, they'll think you don't care about your career. At the end of the day, ignoring your LinkedIn is hurting your ability to earn, and that ability to earn gives you power, which gives you freedom, which gives you the life that you want. It's all connected.

Women want to write LinkedIn off as nothing important: "It's all about who you know." Sure, networking is important, but it's also about how you present yourself to the world.

Sara created a list of accomplishments, including everything that she had participated in that drove revenue for her company, even if she was *just* a team member. Everything was captured on LinkedIn, and then on her résumé, she included more specifics for each item listed on LinkedIn, such as proprietary numbers. So, if she wrote that she grew share of market by 25 percent on her résumé, she put grew share of market by double digits on her LinkedIn.

As she started to list her accomplishments, she began to fully understand all of the great professional milestones she had achieved. With each accomplishment listed, she began to feel more justified in her rage, because she finally realized that she was the common denominator in all of this success. She was the project lead on all of these projects, doing the lion's share of the work and ensuring deadlines were met.

Every time she started to talk negatively about herself, I would have her read through her LinkedIn and remember all of the amazing things she had done. She also read through it when she began negotiations for her salary to remind herself that she was worth her price. Self-doubt wanted to keep her in her cage, but her LinkedIn was visible proof of her value.

I also worked with Sara to research salaries for her position in various locations around the country. Visibility and transparency on what other people are making is empowering for negotiation purposes. Women need to spend a solid amount of time research-ing what market value is for their role in their city. It's also okay to ask other women what they make. Unless we start talking about what we're making, we're never going to close the wage gap.

Just say, "Is it okay if I ask you what you make? Or just a range? I'll tell you what I make too." If you want to start living an incredible life of fulfillment, you have to have money, especially as a trade for the sacrifices you're making to perform that job. You can also approach people who have left the company you are researching. Many people are much more comfortable discussing what they made after they have left.

You have to be your own advocate, and the way to do that is to understand what the potential is for that role in the specific company you are looking for. Women seem to be afraid that there will be retribution or that they'll be called out for "sneaking around" to find out what other people make. First, if there is retribution, that's a *very* clear sign it's time to leave. Second, that is not something to be embarrassed about doing. It's being a self-advocate. People are never going to voluntarily pay you more.

Be sure to protect your base salary. Companies will try to lure you in with a promise of a high bonus—but that is not guaranteed money. They'll quickly find a way out of paying you that bonus, so it's essential that you always protect your base. Tattoo it on yourself if you must.

Note: Every single client mentioned after this point took the first step of updating their LinkedIn. I don't want to bore you by saying it every single time, but I want you to know: every. single. client. updated their LinkedIn first before taking any other professional step. You should too. If you don't know where to start, flip to the Resources section for a LinkedIn cheat sheet.

SARA TODAY

Within two months of us working together, Sara had three different job offers. She chose to move to a woman-owned, midsize tech company. Of course, when she told her old company she was leaving, they begged her to stay, which is what most employers do when they realize they shit the bed with somebody: panic and try to get them back. For a minute, she thought about staying just because it was comfortable. She had tight relationships with the people she managed, and she felt a lot of guilt leaving them behind. But at the end of the day, she had been betrayed by the company.

Betrayal makes it impossible to stay in the situation. Once your company has blatantly lied to you or broken your trust, it's time to go. Past behavior predicts future behavior. They were never going to give her what she needed, so she left.

However, she couldn't make that decision until she had gotten back in tune with herself, through meditation, grounding, and reconnecting with nature. She also looked at herself through the eyes of her daughters. She asked herself, "Would I be cool with it if they were talking to me and telling me what I'm telling Elizabeth? Would I say, 'Yeah, sure, you should stay in that job. That sounds like a great decision'?" She couldn't. She never wanted her daughters to feel what she was feeling.

When she moved to her new company, she added six figures to her base *and* received an additional six figures in stock. She still hasn't lost sight of her dream to start her own company, but at the time, she wasn't quite ready. She still had her kids to think about and bills to pay. But now she's on the right path. Her new job increased her network and is giving her the connections and experience she needs to be able to follow her path.

Sara is now confident, secure, and happy in her job. She's no longer being manipulated into accepting less than she's worth. She needed a fresh start, and now that she has the support she was craving, she's crushing it. In fact, within a year, she was promoted. She's currently exploring starting her own tech company, confident in her skills, worth, and path.

EXPLORE FOR YOURSELF

HONOR THE TWENTY-TWO-YEAR-OLD YOU

Find a picture of you as a young woman when you felt the most powerful, optimistic, and happy. Put that picture somewhere that you'll see it every day, such as on your bathroom mirror or the wall by your desk. Look at her daily and check in with her, because when we're talking about the twenty-two-year-old self, it can feel like that was forever ago or that it's not you anymore.

However, when you look into that picture's eyes and see all of the hope and big plans she had, it's easier to act throughout that day with the intention of making her proud. But, it doesn't have to be you at twenty-two. I recognize that not everyone had a great time in their early twenties. Maybe you were struggling and working three jobs. That's okay. It just needs to be a picture of you at a time in your life when you felt the most alive and the most aligned with your Soul. It could be a picture of you present day, or maybe when you were twelve. The age doesn't matter; the feeling does.

Once you have your picture chosen and hung, try to do a few things each week or month that bring you back to that moment of being excited. For instance, if you had a dream to become a writer, set aside time each week to write.

Next to the picture of you, you can also hang a picture of a strong woman in your life. I have a picture of my paternal grandmother who is a Soul guide for me. My grandmother was a farmer, the OG entrepreneur. The picture I have on my wall is her standing in the ocean with her hands up to the sky. It was the one and only time she rode on a plane and saw the ocean. Now I live in California, and every time I take my girls to frolic in the ocean, I feel her. I know she's living through me, and I can't afford to squander the opportunities and paths she worked so hard to create for me. Every time I look at that picture of my grandma Dorothy, it makes me want to go further, push harder.

We all have opportunities, no matter how small they feel. The key is to start taking one little step toward them. If you're in a low spot and you can't do it for yourself or your children (maybe you don't have children), you can do it for your ancestors. Do it for the strong women in your life who didn't have your opportunities or choices.

My grandmother looks at me from my wall, and every time I have a "this is bullshit" feeling, I look at her—and she looks lovingly back. It's never an "Are you kidding me?" look full of judgment. It's always full of support. She reminds me that I'm not alone. I'm supported by her, my angels, and the Universe. That photograph keeps me on a higher vibrational plane and reminds me that there are beings who are actively rooting me on.

When I first started out and felt a lot of resistance, I had a whole wall that I called "The Wall of Support." I took cards my friends had sent me, pictures of me with my friends, and pictures of me when I was a child with my grandparents, and hung them on the wall of my office in a place where I knew I would look multiple times a day. Any time I was crying, terrified I had made a huge mistake, I would just look at that wall and think of all of those people pulling for me. I couldn't let them down. I couldn't go back to some kind-of-shitty job with some stupid title. I knew that they believed WE were better than that.

For your Wall of Support, include pictures of all the strong people in your life—your kids, clients, coworkers, employees, mentors, and philanthropies—that will all benefit from seeing you financially succeed and your deep personal fulfillment.

WHAT'S THE HARM?

What's the harm in reconnecting with the you who dreamed?

SCREW "HOW?"

HOW TO TRUST (IT'S YOUR ONLY JOB)

"I'm dying to be a part of something special. To have an impact."

—ROBIN

MEET ROBIN

When Robin came to me, she was working for a consulting company and traveling constantly. Like many women who work for consulting agencies, she was burnt out and had zero work–life balance. As she described it, she was circling the drain and wanted out.

Her current company wasn't meeting her standards of what she wanted to make. Everyone gets hung up on money, but Robin in particular was willing to sacrifice her personal life as long as the money was there.

However, she had a secret dream of living in Maui. She had traveled there several times on vacation, staying for two weeks at a time, and she wanted to stay there permanently. At first, she didn't see how she could spend more time there while also working for a demanding company in Los Angeles.

After several discussions, Robin decided to say "fuck 'how?'" and start looking for jobs that weren't meeting her salary requirement but that would give her a better work–life balance. She needed free time so that she could even think about her future. Before we knew it, she had three offers. Two had high salaries but were startups that came with the same amount of work–life balance that she currently had: zero.

Right as the pandemic started, she took the third job offer with a dating app company that added five figures to her base salary and gave her back a life. She also negotiated that she could live in Maui and work remotely. Unfortunately, once the company started bringing people back into the office two years after the pandemic started, they told her she needed to come back to LA.

GUIDING LIGHT: PAM GROUT

"The Universe is limitless, abundant, and strangely accommodating."
—PAM GROUT

Pam Grout's book *E-Squared* not only got me to ask for my orange bus angel sign but its teachings were my touchstone when I had come to a point with this book—the one you're reading—when I wasn't sure if I should write it or not. I was feeling a lot of resistance. My writing coach and super spiritual friend, Rea Frey, reminded me to "just ask for a sign."

In *E-Squared*, Pam reassures us that, at the end of the day, the

Universe has your back and is always trying to help you, but it's okay to ask for proof sometimes in the form of an angel sign.

I had the pleasure of having her as a guest on my podcast, ASCEND and TRANSCEND, and she shared why her book was so influential:

> I think *E-Squared* really hit a chord with people because, while it talked about some of the principles that have been out there forever- I mean, even the Bible says, "Ask and you shall receive." A lot of the books you see out there about this topic are theory. You think this and this will happen. But what I did in this book is I set up these experiments- like scientific experiments- so people can see it with their own two eyes how this works. I think that makes all the difference in the world. It's one thing to give lip service to something, to say, yes, I believe that this is true- but to actually give the universe forty-eight hours to make its presence known just kind of changes it for everybody.

So step number one is identifying what angel sign you want to see, but it can't be an everyday object, such as a red car. There's way too high of a probability that you're going to see a red car in forty-eight hours. Your request has to be very specific. Hence, me asking to see an old-school, orange VW Bus. Next you have to search for it as if it's an item in a scavenger hunt.

Asking for angel signs has become a pillar of the work I do with clients, and over the years they've come up with some pretty interesting ones: a glittery mushroom, a double purple mohawk, a lime-green Kia Soul, a purple dolphin, peacocks—the possibilities are only limited to what your skeptical mind can dream up. That glittery mushroom client: she started seeing them for two straight months when she was on the fence about leaving her job. That's the thing about angel signs: once you ask, you'll get beat over the head with them.

Step number three is once you see your angel sign, even though your rational brain will tell you to chalk it up to coincidence, you need to accept it as proof. That's why your request should be obscure—it's harder for your brain to rationalize it away.

Pam continues:

> There is this cool force that's out there—that really is interacting with you. Always wanting to bless you, guide you…always. And most of us are ignoring it. These experiments jolt you into paying attention, and once you start paying attention, you realize how much is out there and how much we have missed over the years.

Angel signs are the Universe's way of saying you're not in this alone. There's something listening to you other than your Alexa. Imagine the Universe as an anxious, devoted dog. It's sitting by your side, staring up at you with unconditional love, asking you to find a stick (an angel sign), and begging you to throw it so it can bring it back to you. It's just sitting there enthusiastically waiting and waiting and waiting, trembling with anticipation for you to give it an opportunity to prove it's there, but because we don't see the "dog" on this physical plane, we never throw the "stick."

IGNORING REALITY

Reality is a control mechanism. Everybody says, "Be realistic," but there is no reality. It's all subjective, and it's all evolving. Another common saying is, "Your thoughts create your reality." Instead, it should be, "Thoughts create present conditions." The emotions you feel at the present moment are creating your current reality.

The key takeaway is to let the Universe make the path. We have the wheel, but the Universe is going to present you with the best path forward. All you have to know—scratch that, *feel*—is that the path in front of you is for your highest good—no matter how ugly, destructive, or painful it may look.

SPIRITUAL STEPS

Robin's main angel signs were crows and repeating numbers. However, before she could ask for a sign, she had to create space in her life to actually see the signs. She made it a point to leave her apartment and get out into the world so she could notice them. She started creating that elusive "work–life" balance (going to yoga, hanging out with friends, going to events), and once she wasn't 100 percent focused on work, she was able to notice her angel's messages.

The biggest sign, however, always came when she was in Maui. Every time she was there, she felt like she was in total Soul alignment—basically living in an angel sign.

When people feel immediately calm and at home in a city or space, it's a huge message that they are in alignment with their spiritual board of advisors. It's how I felt in California. I knew it was my spiritual home and I had to live here. Robin recognized that and made it a priority to live there full time.

Your angel sign doesn't have to be a physical thing. If you don't see a purple dolphin, it doesn't mean that your angels aren't speaking to you. Deep, powerful waves of feelings can be your sign, especially when they are around decisions.

But when you are first starting out with your angel signs, it's okay to ask to see physical signs. Once you begin trusting in them, you can rely and trust in these waves of immense feelings when they come. Eventually, you'll get to the point that you don't need to see angel signs. You still will, of course, but they'll become little nods from your angels letting you know they're still there. You'll trust that when you feel good, you are in alignment, and there is an open avenue for them to send you messages, disguised as your feelings.

PROFESSIONAL STEPS

Robin's first step was to network, network, network. She went through her personal Rolodex and started calling, emailing, and texting everyone she had worked with over the last five to ten years—and she had a lot of names thanks to her background in consulting.

She also reached out to friends and family. In the end, it was a friend who got her the interview for the job she chose. However, the people you network with don't have to be close friends. It can be someone you met once at a party and then see on LinkedIn that they work for the company you are interested in.

All it takes is one person: someone who can make that introduction or be a reference that gets your résumé to the top of the pile. Make a list of the people you are friends with, or even just acquainted with, people you've worked with in the past, and people you've worked for in the past. Then, make a list of the companies you aspire to work for, look at the companies on LinkedIn, and see if anyone you know works at, or has a mutual connection with, that company.

LinkedIn's algorithm will show you mutual connections when you scroll the people tab on a company's page. If you don't have a single mutual connection, look for someone who went to the same university or is in one of the same groups on LinkedIn as you. Look hard for any point of connection you have within that company.

In the worst-case scenario where you don't know anyone who knows anyone who works for that company, you aren't out of luck yet.

Say you want to work for a smaller tech company. Look at your original list and see if you know anyone who works for a similar company. Reach out to that person and see who they know in the industry.

In all industries, somebody knows somebody who works there, and that is all you need. It's powerful to get an introduction to the hiring manager or recruiter because it immediately puts you at the very top of the candidate pool. Most jobs come from people who know someone who works there rather than recruiters.

It's okay if you don't think you have a big network to lean on. There are a few different ways to start. The easiest way—that's free—is to use LinkedIn. First, get your LinkedIn really polished. Once you're ready to make a good first impression, do some LinkedIn sleuthing. Look at the companies you want to work for and see if you have any existing connections there.

If you don't, start reaching out to friends. For really good friends, you can send them an email saying, "Hey, you know what? I'm exploring new opportunities and I really want to work at Vans. I know you live in Southern California; do you know anyone who works there?" This only works with a warm contact, someone who is not going to think, *Who is this person?* when they get your email.

If they're not a warm contact, such as someone you haven't talked to in a few years, only talk to sporadically, or if you're not sure they'll remember you, reach out through LinkedIn's messaging system. However, before you hit send on that direct message, look at their profile and see their activity. Maybe they're someone who never posts. If so, they're going to be hard to connect with.

If they have posted in the last two or three weeks, go click on that post (which will be listed in their activity feed) and comment on it. Congratulate them on a promotion. Tell them how valued and relevant their insights are on an article they shared. Don't just "like" the post, and don't leave a one-word comment. Put thought into it.

This immediately turns a cold contact warm because now you've done something for them. You gave them a compliment or you shared their content in your feed. Generally, people will reply to your comment within a few days. Once a week goes by with no reply, you can then reach out and say, "Hey, I was thinking about the XYZ post you made, and I'd love to reconnect." Alternatively, you can cut straight to the point and send, "Hey, I see that you work at ABC company. I would love to get your insights on what the culture is there, because I've always wanted to work with them."

Next, write some recommendations. These can be kind words about how a past boss, client, or colleague made you feel, showed up to projects, or overcame obstacles. It's a wonderful way to get yourself front of mind with a person who may have forgotten about you, and an opener to have a chat about opportunities they may know of.

Don't ask them to get you a job right off the jump, however. Ease them into the relationship. As a bonus, you get to learn more about the company you are interested in from a firsthand account. Find anyone who will give you ten minutes to talk about culture. Then, while you are on the call, you can ask, "Do you happen to know about any opportunities?" Or, if you see an open job posting on LinkedIn, you can say, "Hey, I saw this open position. If it's something you'd feel comfortable with, can I give you my résumé to pass directly to the hiring manager?"

Usually they'll say yes, because most companies give kickbacks. If you get hired as a referral of theirs, they can get anywhere from $200–$2,000. The knowledge that you are also helping them can help you overcome the notion that you're being annoying. "I don't want to bother anyone": bother away because you are going to help them get paid.

ROBIN TODAY

Robin knew that she didn't want to move back to LA full time. The difference was that now she was at the point where she trusted the Universe to manifest the right opportunity for her. She didn't even have to put forth any effort. She had already followed the professional and spiritual steps, so once she decided she wanted to leave the company, she was inundated with recruiter requests.

Once again, she received three offers. One would give her no work–life balance, would pay her a lot of money, but was also in LA. The second was a consulting job that would pay her more than she was making and let her stay in Maui. The third was with a consulting company, which would pay her about the same but let her live wherever she wanted.

In the end, Robin chose the first offer but negotiated another six figures onto her base, along with the stipulation that she could live nine months out of the year in Maui. And in early 2022, she was promoted to a C-Suite position in the company.

When she stopped trying to control the process, she realized that the right support would show up at the right time. Now, she believes that the spiritual plane will figure everything out and put the right opportunities in front of her. She only has to stick to her value system and choose the right one.

EXPLORE FOR YOURSELF: GET YOUR GUIDES OFF THE BENCH

1. Identify the question you want to ask.
2. Choose an angel sign.
3. Look for it, hard. Like it's a scavenger hunt.
4. Accept it—override your rational brain that will come in and try to discount it.
5. Embrace this tool and use it often.

You don't have to ask to see angel signs only for big decisions, like *Should I leave my spouse?* or *Should I switch careers?* It can be for anything: Where should we go on vacation? Is this a good person to be friends with? Is now a good time to move? Is this coworker somebody that I should trust?

It can be super small in the beginning. In fact, you may *need* it to be small in the beginning. If you start out the gate with *Should I leave my spouse?*, it might be too big of a bridge for your rational mind to cross once you get your first sign.

I can hear you saying, "Well *your* first request was a big one." It was. I asked, "Am I going to be okay? Am I doing the right thing by starting this business?" The difference was my headspace. I was already super open to spiritual signs because I had spent eight years of learning how. This was just the first concrete visual I got along with a feeling.

Once you choose your angel sign, you need to have patience when looking for it. So many people will look for twenty-four to forty-eight hours, then say, "I told you I don't have one. I haven't seen it in forty-eight hours. It doesn't work." That is the Universe testing you to make you be more patient. A big piece of this is not losing faith, and thinking instead, "I guess the Universe needs more time." Once you commit to patience, you'll see it. If you put any sort of parameters on your sign request that are too tight, the Universe might make you hold out a little longer.

Also, remember you don't have to be the one to see the sign. One example I love is with a client who asked to see a double purple mohawk. Just from that request, you can tell this woman was very skeptical. She went forty-eight hours and didn't see it. Later that day, I was at the Santa Monica Pier and I saw a performer who had, no joke, two purple mohawks. I took a picture, sent it to her, and said, "Oh my God, here it is." She replied, "It doesn't count because *you* saw it. *I* didn't see it." (I told you, skeptical.) So I said, "You're seeing it now though, aren't you? Through the picture I sent you?" When she finally admitted yes, I told her, "Then *you* saw it."

She, like so many others, wanted to prove the Universe wrong. They're trying to prove that nobody has their back, they have bad luck, it's not going to work for them. That's your ego brain talking. It's not your Spirit. Your Spirit wants to see these things. Your Spirit is the one that gave you the idea to read this book. However, this resistance—which really is your ego—comes in and tries to put the brakes on because it doesn't want you to grow. It wants you to stay mediocre and low-key miserable because that's what it thinks is safe. During this exercise, resistance will pop up to say, "I kind of hope it happens, but I almost equally hope it doesn't." Push through, and keep asking.

You don't have to have just one angel sign that you use for everything. There can be all sorts of little comforts. You can ask to see a bus one time, a purple mohawk the next, or your late grandmother's favorite animal. Just be open to any message. I once saw a personalized license plate that said, "LIZRELX." Liz relax, right in front of me on a day when I really needed to relax.

In the beginning, treat everything good as a sign. Don't go out looking to disprove your signs. You also can't overdo asking for signs. There's no police that is going to come and say, "Excuse me, you're asking too much from your angels." It's impossible to exhaust them. Use them, trust them, and act on them. Let them bring you the comfort and peace you deserve.

EXAMPLES OF ANGEL SIGNS

Drawing a blank on what to ask for as an angel sign? Here are some angel signs that my clients have asked to see to get you started:

- Orange VW Bus (obviously)
- Double purple mohawk
- Glittery mushroom
- Purple dolphin
- Dachshund dog
- Peacock
- Flamingo
- Blue butterflies
- White feathers
- Coins
- Repeating numbers

IT'S AN INSIDE JOB

HOW TO LET GO OF THE IDEA
MATERIAL THINGS BRING HAPPINESS

"I'm hanging on by a thread."

—JENNIFER

MEET JENNIFER

Jennifer owns a marketing agency in Park City, Utah. Her company was thriving, but on our first call, she was huddled up in the corner of her kids' bedroom on the floor, laptop resting on her knees, wearing a winter knit hat. Right outside her door, you could hear her kids raging, because lockdown had just started and school was closed. Her first words were, "I'm hanging on by a thread." I believed her. She *looked* like she was hanging on by a thread. She needed to take a breath.

I asked her, "When was the last time you went skiing?" The Park City area is big on skiing. Her kids went to ski school every day, and her husband skied most days too, even though he works for her agency. Jennifer, however, hadn't been skiing in four years. I asked, "Do you like to ski?" She said, "Oh, I love it." When I asked why she wasn't skiing then, she said, "There's just too much work to do." Her reasoning for working herself to the bone was that she wanted the "stuff" for her and her family. I didn't want to push her too hard, too fast, so on that first call, I let it slide.

When I say Jennifer was obsessed with working, I mean she hadn't so much as taken a beat for self-care in over five years. She was teetering on nervous breakdown territory, because she was addicted to the busy-ness—to her it'd become a badge of honor. Over a few sessions, we started to dig into what happened five years ago that triggered her work addiction.

It took until our sixth session for her to tell me that she had a baby who died three days after it was born. She wasn't just avoiding that unbearable pain, she was *sprinting* away from it. Addicted to work, her devices, and her children's schedules, she thought that if she stopped for even a minute, she may be destroyed by the pain.

GUIDING LIGHT: THICH NHAT HANH

"My actions are my only true belongings. I cannot escape the consequences of my actions. My actions are the ground upon which I stand."

—THICH NHAT HANH

Thich Nhat Hanh's main principle is that everything is always changing. If you feel good right now, that will change. If you feel bad right now, that will change. The prompting of change is when conditions are no longer set towards what you want.

He gives the example of a match. Before it's lit, the match is not fire and also not, not fire. The condition of striking the match is what needs to happen in order for the fire to manifest, but the fire itself was never not there. There was always the potential of the fire. Then, when conditions no longer support the match being lit, it will go out, but that fire is still always there.

My novice takeaway from Hanh is that everything we want is always right there in front of us, we just have to wait for the proper conditions for it to manifest into a visible and physical representation. For Jennifer (and all of us, too), the things that she wanted to manifest in physical form were always there. All that was needed was the patience to wait for the conditions to be right. The peaceful life experience she wanted was always there; she simply needed to get on the mountain to feel it.

When we're feeling less than, trapped, or filled with self-doubt, we'll never be able to manifest externally the things we want. It's hard to create internal change when you're distracted by social media and online shopping. Until you can find some way to be still, you'll never truly understand what internal conditions you're working with.

PRE-STEP

With Jennifer, before she could take any professional or spiritual steps, she needed to address her internal pain. We started by talking about the baby. We said her name multiple times. We discussed that because she was an angel now, she was a wonderful asset. According to clients of past-life regression expert Michael Newton, PhD, souls sometimes sign up for a short life, knowing they're going to be a miscarriage or knowing that they're going to die early in their lives. The reason as to why is vast but his research found that "Souls of young children who die soon after birth often return to the same parents as the soul of their next baby. These plans are made in advance by the souls participating in the tragic family events." The "lesson" is often for the parents.

Basically, he explains that when souls choose to return for a short life it's to help someone else rather than work on their own issues. If there is a premature death, it's likely they volunteered in advance for those bodies.

We worked to get Jennifer to a place of peace knowing that nothing she did while she was pregnant could have changed the outcome. This was the whole life journey of that baby. The baby was there to either show her something that she didn't want to look at, teach her something, or even just send her love for the nine months she was pregnant.

To slowly ease her out of running from her pain, she started skiing with her husband. In the beginning, she only went out once a week, but even then, she immediately felt better. Anyone who skis knows that it can be fun, but you have to be very present or else you could die. There's a popular saying that downhill skiers stay present and focus only on the path, because if you focus on the trees, that's where you're going to end up.

We used the same tactic with Jennifer. We had to get her on the skis to be present, focusing on the path, not on the trees (the pain) that she was trying to avoid. Slowly but surely, she started to feel like herself again.

SPIRITUAL STEPS

Once she was feeling more centered, she could start taking spiritual and professional steps. List-making can be a powerful spiritual tool, so I had Jennifer write down all of the things she wanted.

First, she wanted a new car. She had been driving the same Suburban for over five years, because she was responsible for driving her three kids to activities and events. Her husband, of course, drove something smaller and nicer. She wrote down *a new car* on her list, and then wrote down all the other things she wanted. Once her list was complete, we went through it together and wrote what feeling getting each item would give her.

For Jennifer, the new car was going to make her feel like all of her hard work, both for the family and for the company, was validated and that she had earned it. In reality, she could have gone out and bought whatever car she wanted that day. She was the one holding the carrot of a new car in front of her to manipulate herself to work harder.

Often when you make a list and you closely examine what you want and why, it can be enlightening.

If your list includes material possessions, that's one thing. If it's acclaim, why? Many writers want to be a *New York Times* bestselling author. That's great, but what are you searching for? Why do you want to be seen? Usually it's because you want to be validated that you're smart or that you have something to offer the world. At the end of the day, wanting all of the material gain or acclaim is just a way to try to convince yourself that you have worth. Because if you have the things that everybody says is of X amount of value, then *you* will have that value.

It's fine to have desires. It's fine to want a nice car that's safe and keeps you warm in the snow. However, if you want it just to build up your worth, then it's probably best to give it up at that moment. As Thich Nhat Hanh would say, there's nothing that you can do or buy that adds to your worth or detracts from it. So why are we chasing material things?

When you make your own list and assign a feeling to each item, take a look at the most repetitive feelings. Feelings such as pride, value, and worthiness are all ego based. Not ego as in "I drive a Porsche and I'm an egomaniac," but ego as in our internal thought guidance system.

Ego is our survival brain, not our Spirit. Eckhart Tolle's book *A New Earth* explains:

> The ego isn't wrong; it's just unconscious. When you observe the ego in yourself, you are beginning to go beyond it. Don't take the ego too seriously. When you detect egoic behavior in yourself, smile. At times you may even laugh. How could humanity have been taken in by this for so long? Above all, know that the ego isn't personal. It isn't who you are. If you consider the ego to be your personal problem, that's just more ego.

To me that means when we feel those egoic feelings, it's a clue we are listening to the wrong part of ourselves and we're no longer in alignment with our Souls.

PROFESSIONAL STEPS

Jennifer's first professional step was to assess each person on her team, because she needed to understand why she felt like she couldn't delegate to them. As we talked through each member of the team, she would say, "They're great. I can tell them to do something and it gets done." When I dug further, however, I found that she would give a project to an employee and if it wasn't done within a day, she'd take the project back and say, "I'll just do it myself. It'll be faster."

That is a terrible example of leadership to set for your company. Every time she took a project back from them, she reinforced the idea that she didn't trust them and wasn't going to let them grow.

Jennifer needed to manage her expectations and understand that for her to have the life she wanted, she had to start delegating to her team—a team that was ready, willing, and able. They were excited to take on more work. They wanted more responsibility, as most good employees do. Instead, Jennifer was burning herself out trying to do everything herself. She needed to understand that it's like a child wanting to tie their own shoe. It's going to be painful watching them do it the first time, but you have to let them do it and show them you have faith in their ability.

Once Jennifer saw how she was treating her team from this new perspective, realized that the message she was sending to them was the opposite of how she truly felt about them, and figured out it was a win–win so she could go skiing with her husband and start to heal her wounds, she started to delegate. She let them tackle big projects and client meetings by themselves.

She stopped micromanaging and her team rose to the challenge beautifully. In fact, they thrived. And Jennifer was able to disconnect more from the work that she had become addicted to.

I've seen many women fall into this same trap in their relationships, especially moms. "I do everything for my kids because I know my partner's not going to do it right." Just because they are going to do it differently than you doesn't mean it's the wrong way. A peanut butter and jelly sandwich with different jelly and the crust still on won't kill your kid.

We disempower people when we swoop in and try to save the day or do it the "right" way. Look at your entire support network, both at work and at home, and see who is trying to help you, who really wants to offer support. It could be someone you've shot down so many times they've given up. You may be able to reengage them by saying, "I'm sorry that in the past I never let you do it your way. I agree to allow you to do things your way this time, if we can agree on some basic expectations." Communicate what your expectations are and then detach. Let them take over and trust them to follow through.

JENNIFER TODAY

It's probably no surprise that Jennifer's agency is still at the top of its game, but the difference is that she's now living with a sense of peace that everything happened for a reason, and everything currently *is* happening for a reason. When she was focused on getting material things, she was trying to bury the pain because the work wasn't numbing it anymore. It's a common tactic for most people that when work stops numbing the pain, they'll focus on gaining material things to try to bury it.

It's not all sunshine and roses, however. She still struggles with backsliding into workaholic tendencies. But now, she sees another path where she has the time and freedom to breathe. Even if you back-slide to the bad path, you'll now know that there's always another option, and you can choose whether you go back and forth versus feeling like you're heading towards the trees.

EXPLORE FOR YOURSELF: HABIT TRACK

Jennifer, like so many women, needed a visual to see how she was actually spending her day. She was astounded at how much of her time was spent on work-related tasks. Once you see your day in black and white, it can be really eye opening.

When I say habit tracker, you probably are thinking about a list full of little boxes you can check off: exercise thirty minutes, check. Read a book for ten minutes, check. However, this needs to focus on how much time you are spending working, thinking about work, or dreaming about work. How much sleep are you losing?

So many women will say, "I worked out thirty minutes today, so that's my me-time done." And the rest of their day is spent giving to their family and their employer. At the end of the day, thirty minutes for yourself is pathetic. It's nowhere near what you deserve.

Visit my website for a free habit tracker PDF download.

WHAT'S THE HARM?

What's the harm in believing you are enough *without* material things?

THE REAL
F-BOMB: FEAR

HOW TO REMOVE THE
HANDCUFFS OF SELF-DOUBT

"I'm beyond burned out. In fifteen minutes I'm boarding a seventeen-hour flight to India and have to work the whole time."

—HANNAH

MEET HANNAH

When Hannah reached out, she was working for a large manufacturer in the health sector, and she was technically based in Maryland.

However, she was on planes Monday through Friday, every week, often flying out on Sundays to be on location by Monday morning. She joined the company right after graduation and had already moved eight times for them. She would move, live in the new city for four or five months, and then they'd reassign her to another city. But even after she moved, she was traveling weekly to go to other cities to check on operations. Basically, they were running her ragged.

However, in her immaturity right out of college, this looked like success to her. She thought she should be grateful to be a "road warrior." Being a road warrior looks flashy and fun, getting lots of miles and tons of hotel points. It fuels your ego. Knowing someone is paying you to fly to all these places means you must be important. The reality is: it's lonely. Hannah kept being chosen to travel because other coworkers would refuse on the grounds they had families (and boundaries). Hannah's mindset was: "I'm going to run, run, run, because this is what society and my parents have told me success looks like."

Unfortunately, it wasn't just affecting her—it was affecting her relationships too. She couldn't hold onto a romantic partner because the men she dated wouldn't put up with the fact she was never home. She wanted to join a kickball league and a yoga studio, but she couldn't because she was never home. All of the memberships would be completely wasted. When she was home, she was exhausted, so all she was up for was cuddling with her two greyhounds.

Hannah was being lured in by the money, the ego drive of being busy, and the status of being flown around. She had external pressures too. As an only child, her mother had unrealistic standards for her. As a result, a very loud voice grew in her head saying she needed to keep living this life, because her mother wouldn't understand if she left a "good" job.

When she was traveling, she had to leave her dogs, and they were

her "babies." Traveling meant being away from the one unconditional source of love she had in her life, Monday through Friday,
twenty days a month.

On our first call, she was sitting in a Delta lounge, getting ready
to travel to India, with a seventeen-hour flight in front of her. I
asked what she needed help with, and Hannah said, "I'm running
nonstop, and I feel like I'm not in control of where I'm running
to." This was a typical case of somebody teetering on burnout
and feeling out of control. When you feel out of control in your
career, you feel out of control in your life.

We started talking about what she really wanted out of life. She
wanted the dream: meet somebody, get married, buy a house,
have kids (she already had the dogs). However, she knew that if
she wasn't able to stay put in one place that none of that was ever
going to manifest. We had a great introductory call, and then she
had seventeen hours to think about what her next step was. As
soon as she landed in India, she emailed me and said that she was
ready to take action. She was done being unfulfilled even though
she was doing everything you were *supposed* to do.

GUIDING LIGHT: STEVEN PRESSFIELD

*"Are you paralyzed with fear? That's a good sign. Fear is good. Like
self-doubt, fear is an indicator. Fear tells us what we have to do.
Remember one rule: the more scared we are of a work or calling, the
more sure we can be that we have to do it."*

—STEVEN PRESSFIELD

Once you can understand resistance—when it shows up, what it
looks like when it shows up, what it feels like, and the lies that it

tells you—you can disarm it. Unfortunately, many people don't understand the concept of resistance. They confuse resistance with their intuition or their gut trying to protect them. There's a big difference between your gut (aka your Soul) trying to protect you and resistance.

You may *think* your Soul is telling you, "You can't have a new life," but that's not your Soul speaking—that's fear. The first step is to be able to distinguish what is resistance and what is your Soul's guidance.

It's easy to identify something as resistance if it comes when you're trying to grow. According to Pressfield, anytime you try to grow spiritually or professionally—anytime you try to lose weight, anytime you try to better yourself or expand—resistance will show up. Fear is different. Fear is false evidence appearing real: the voice telling you to stay in your same shitty relationship, in your same shitty town, or in your same shitty job. A good litmus test is to ask, is it a feeling or message that is cautioning against you growing or bettering yourself in some way? If it is, that's resistance, not your Soul.

Now you could also have a similar scenario where you are going to move, but it's to a place you never saw yourself living, with a guy who doesn't treat you well. That's not resistance. That's your Soul saying this isn't for your highest good.

Resistance can come in when you're excited about something too, and it becomes your Debbie Downer. For example, say you're excited about writing a book. Debbie Downer, your resistance, will come in and say, "Yeah, you'll never get that published. No one is ever going to read it. You'll never finish it anyway." Don't listen to Debbie Downer. Lean into the resistance, and do the thing anyway.

SPIRITUAL STEPS

Hannah implemented the Law of Assumption to attract her dream life. You've likely heard all about the Law of Attraction, which happens when you think deeply about what you want, and make it your focal point in order to draw it in. But the Law of Assumption is a bit different. It is about acting as if you already have the things you want to manifest. It's you getting into character. Think about method actors, who become their character in order to give the best performance. It's the same with manifestation. You have to start acting like the person you want to be right now.

To be clear, this doesn't mean that if you want to be a millionaire that you should go and max out your credit cards buying things you can't afford. It's about putting yourself in situations that *feel* like what you want to manifest so your mind will start to believe it's possible.

When I first started using the Law of Assumption, I would go to fancy resorts where I felt like I didn't belong. I would see families buying thirty-five-dollar hamburgers for their kids without flinching and think, *I am in the wrong place. They can see from a mile away that I do not belong here. I would never bring my children to a place this expensive.*

But it was the type of place I wanted to feel I belonged in, so I started going more and more. I started bringing my laptop with me and working in the lobby even though it felt uncomfortable. I would wait for someone to walk up, point at me, and say, "Let me see your net worth"—and then kick me out. Of course, no one ever did.

I would buy a seven-dollar cup of coffee and work there for hours, watching the people coming in, and aspire to get to a "no scarcity" mindset. It took practice—paying the thirty-dollar valet fee didn't feel great in the beginning—but I kept telling myself, "I belong here. I am just like all of these people. Someday I will bring my family here and not flinch at buying a thirty-five-dollar burger for my child who is going to eat a single bite."

Act like the life you want is on its way to manifesting. It's already in your vortex: you're just in the process of accessing it. If you need more reminders, write "It's on its way" on Post-it Notes and stick them in all of the high-traffic areas of your house so you have to remember that what you want is on its way.

PROFESSIONAL STEPS

Before Hannah could find a new job, she needed to know where she wanted to work. Even though her current job was in the healthcare industry, she knew she wanted to make a pivot into fashion and retail. To start, we created a basic Excel tracker of her dream employers, which tracked:

- Companies she wanted to work for
- Contacts she had in that company
- The last time she reached out to that contact
- Hyperlinks of viable job postings

Essentially, this spreadsheet was the hub that contained all the information that had to do with her job search. Hannah identified that she wanted to move to Austin, so she researched companies that had a headquarters or office in that city and focused on those first, rather than letting whatever jobs were available dictate where she would live.

After she did all her research, Hannah listed out all of the companies headquartered in Austin and chose the one she was most excited about. Once she knew where she wanted to go, she updated her LinkedIn to be more curated toward that employer, even going as far as to change her location to Austin. Every skill is transferable, and if you can communicate well enough, you can connect the dots for recruiters from your current job to your hopeful job.

By this point, she really believed that she could work for her identified dream companies. She was excited and hopeful, which raised her vibration, and before she knew it, she was interviewing with them—and then got a fabulous job…in Austin.

Hannah understood and believed that nothing was out of her wheelhouse. Same goes for you. When people tell you to stay in your lane, they're spewing bullshit because they feel threatened. You being fearless can make others feel insecure or intimidated because they are too afraid to do the same. Hannah refused to listen, broke out of her cage, and has never looked back. Now she has a more well-rounded career portfolio versus a linear career path, which could have led her into another career cage.

HANNAH TODAY

Not only did Hannah land the job but she found a wonderful roommate to cover half the mortgage on her new home. She also met a wonderful guy, and they fell in love. Everything she had wanted, she got, and it was because she overcame the fear and took a big, scary step and moved. Sometimes you have to take that huge leap of faith, especially if there's a financial component tied to it.

Finances are the number one thing that will keep people confined. They stay in the fear—in the resistance—because they think the money won't work out. Hannah felt that fear too, but we talked through the worst that could happen. Maybe she had to ask her parents for help with the mortgage payment if she didn't find a roommate in time. But that was unlikely, because everything was starting to lock down thanks to the pandemic, and people wanted out of their tiny apartments. Hannah lived in a beautiful, newly built home; the odds of not finding anyone who wanted more space in lockdown was very slim.

In the beginning, Hannah was stuck in a hole and couldn't see the light to find her way out. But once she started leaning into her fear, seeing it as a cue to what she needed to do, she was able to take small action steps to free herself. These little steps gave her momentum, and now she's one of the most fearless people I know. She's started a side hustle coaching recent graduates on their next steps, so they don't become stuck like her.

She believed the Universe would show up, even when she couldn't see it or feel it. Every step wasn't easy. When she was buying the house, the contractor tried to swindle her. There were delays in the closing. There were obstacles that popped up every step of the way, but she stayed committed to the decision to move, because she knew that was where her life was going to be. She trusted in the Universe, asked for angel signs to give her green lights, and held on to her confidence. Now she has the life she wanted in the city she wanted.

EXPLORE FOR YOURSELF: FACE THE DRAGON

When you feel fear, the best advice I can give you is to face the dragon: write out your worst-case scenarios. Often, the worst-case scenario isn't as bad as you think it is, or it's something that is exceptionally improbable. Many people think they're going to end up under a bridge with their family, when, in reality, there are a *lot* of steps that have to happen before you end up there. Most of us have family members who would let us couch surf for a month, even with our kids. But our minds go to the worst-case scenario, and we use that excuse to not take action.

Think about an action you want to take. Then, think of your worst-case scenario. Write out every single step that would have to happen before you would get to that worst-case scenario. Once you've written it out, you can see how unrealistic the scenario is, so you can silence Debbie when she tries to bring it up. If you need to go a step further, when you're writing out all the worst-case scenario steps, you can also write out steps you can take to counteract it.

If your scenario is "I can't make a mortgage payment," you could look at what it would take to get a loan or talk to your parents. Say, "I'm going to make this move. Do you have savings in case I can't make my first month's mortgage payment?" People want to help other people. Crowdfunding is always an option if living under a bridge feels likely to happen. Most of us underestimate how much our friends and families would be there for us when we need them. Making these plans helps you see that you do have safety nets and won't end up under the bridge.

And don't discount the other possibility: what if everything goes right?

Once you finish your list of doom, list out a parallel timeline of the steps that you need to take to get to the amazing goal or dream life that you want. That's what you focus on. Take your doomsday timeline about all the things that could go wrong and rip it up, burn it, or put it in a drawer in case you "need" it—whatever is most cathartic. Take the steps to reach your goal and hang them where you can see them. The main point is to focus on the preferred outcome that is worth overcoming this fear to get.

When you are able to see that your fears are unlikely to happen, you let yourself get your hopes up. That raises your vibration and helps manifest those hopes.

WHAT'S THE HARM?

What's the harm in believing that your Spirit is not a Debbie Downer?

THE BIG MOVE

ESCAPING GEOGRAPHICAL CONFINEMENT

My move to California was the scariest thing I've ever done in my life.

Once my husband, Ryan, and I decided we needed to live in Cali, we trusted it was "on the way" and were okay with whatever timeline it took to get us here. We knew staying in Chicago for the rest of our lives was not going to be good for our marriage or where we envisioned Delilah and Vivi growing up (I wanted them to be able to go outside more than three or four months a year). We set the intention, let go, and the Universe started moving things along.

The small company Ryan worked for was sold to a larger company, and he had been given a role managing the Midwest division. Having gone to so many work parties and events, I kept asking about his coworkers—what was happening to them? Did they have spots in the new company too? Ryan told me many had offers, but they'd have to relocate to San Francisco. I said, "Wait, they're relo-ing people? Have you looked to see if there are any openings in California?"

Ryan said, "Well, no."

"But we said we were going there."

"I didn't think you were serious. Really?"

"I am dead fucking serious."

"Okay, let me look." The next day Ryan said there was a state manager job for California, but it was over two divisions, one of which was the biggest money-maker for the company. I told him he should go for it, even though he wasn't the most confident he could get the role. He told me there were fourteen other people interviewing for it, and a lot of them were internal people who had been there for years. Jobs like this didn't open up a lot. I said, "It doesn't matter. You have to interview. If it doesn't work out, fine, but it feels like the Universe is trying to help us." To me, it seemed as if the Universe was trying to say, here's the job: you can either go for it or stay where you are.

I could see that Ryan was hesitant. I think he was hoping I was going to say, "On second thought, this probably isn't the right time because we have a two- and a four-year-old." Plus, his parents were close by and came over all the time—hello, free babysitting.

He couldn't understand why we would leave everything that we had in Illinois just because of the weather. He kept saying, "We can just vacation a lot more. Let's go on more vacations." I didn't want to go on vacation. I wanted to *live* in a vacation spot. So, a bit begrudgingly, he interviewed—and made it to the next round. And then he kept making it to the next round. And you bet that in between, I was coaching him like crazy and upgrading his LinkedIn profile.

Eventually, he went to San Francisco to interview and made it to the final round. It was terrifying, because it meant shit was getting real. If he got the job, we were going to have to move. And then, he got it. The entire situation was like being on a waterbed; we couldn't get stable. Every time we cleared one hurdle, there was another. We negotiated salary. Then, we negotiated relocation.

As part of the relo package, they gave us two paid trips to house hunt. We had decided we wanted to live in San Francisco, one, because we loved San Francisco, and two, because I thought that was where all of the smart, "woke" people lived. My understanding of Orange County was what I saw on Bravo, which looked shallow and vapid so I didn't want to live there. However, everyone kept telling me, "Northern California is not great weather. It's gloomy, it's rainy, and you won't like it." I said, "I don't care. It's where the smart, liberal people are. That's where we're going."

We went our allotted two times and even with a generous seven-figure house budget, every place we saw was a dump. They didn't have garages, they didn't have sidewalks, and the schools were horrible. We'd go out with the real estate agent and I'd start crying walking into these "grandma" houses. Eventually, I stopped getting out of the car at all. (The real estate agent didn't know what to do with me.)

One night, after a long, frustrating day of looking and crying, we went to dinner at a nice restaurant, which happened to be one of Ryan's new accounts, and we ran into a table full of men who were going to be his new boss' bosses. They could see I was upset at first glance (the running makeup and red, puffy eyes were probably a dead giveaway), and they were extremely kind. They said, "Don't worry. If San Francisco isn't a fit, why not look at Southern California?" We explained that we'd committed to San Francisco, and they had negotiated his salary based on us living there versus SoCal. Yet, they did their best to reassure us that everything would work out.

Ryan and I talked it over, and I told him he had to negotiate for us to move to Southern California, *and* we needed them to give us another trip, on their dime, to go house hunting. His boss was incredible and gave us a paid trip to SoCal, telling Ryan, "If that feels like it's a better fit, we can go back and adjust whatever we need to."

People say living in SoCal is like living behind the orange curtain—for good reason. It's always sunny and beautiful here all. the.time. Yes, there are people who look like they've been caught in a wind tunnel because they've tucked and pulled their faces so much, and there are more Lamborghinis here than I've ever seen in my life, but the weather, homes, and schools were exactly what we were looking for. It was a wave of relief. His company was more than okay with us moving to SoCal, and they didn't even reduce his salary.

It was time to tell his family the news, and it wasn't easy. His parents immediately started crying. His sister told us she was pregnant and possibly buying a house that was a few blocks away from the house we were actively selling. We could feel the resistance piling on. My best friend lived next door, and my sister was only a short twenty-minute drive. They were bummed I was moving thousands of miles away. I'm not sure they really understood why someone who seemingly had the perfect life would need more. Why couldn't I be happy where I was?

Yet, there was something inside me pulling and saying, "You cannot stay here. There is more for you, and you owe it to yourself and your kids to see it." I'm not going to lie: it was hard to move, really hard. There were so many days I wondered if we had made a huge mistake. I was constantly second-guessing. After we landed in SoCal with nothing but our small children and a pile of suitcases, Ryan and I looked at each other, and I knew we were thinking the same thing: *What the fuck have we gotten ourselves into?*

At this point, we didn't have a house. We didn't have a school. We didn't have a babysitter. Instead, we had corporate housing, which turned out to be the dingiest, grossest apartment I had ever been in. There were toenails in the bathtub, it was cold and dirty, and I cried the first night, thinking we had made a huge mistake. Thankfully, Ryan kept a level head, called the company, and got us out of there a short week later. He found us a nice Airbnb that we were able to rent month to month.

As you may have guessed, we hit resistance there too. The day we were moving into the Airbnb—I was literally putting together a crib for Vivian—when I overheard the landlord downstairs say, "You can't stay here. I can't rent to you anymore. There's another family who came earlier and their house flooded, so I rented it to them." I remember falling to my knees, because my first thought was, *Now we're literally homeless.* Ryan was downstairs with him and said, "No. You're renting to us, sign this." After some (assertive) back and forth, he signed it, and we stayed there for three months.

During those three months, we put bids in on four different homes—and got outbid every time. Then, a house came on the market that was way overpriced and out of our budget. In my mind, it was a total gut-job. However, the Universe had closed all these other doors and made it impossible to find a house—until this one. This house had been on the market for four weeks. It needed a new kitchen, a new pool, a new everything. We ended up being able to get it for $30,000 under ask, and asked his company for an extra month on our corporate housing, allowing us to start renovations before we moved in. It turned out to be the best house we've ever lived in. We have amazing neighbors, it's in the best school district, we can see the ocean from our couch, and I love every inch of it.

Nowadays, I never doubt the Universe. It was taking care of us all along, getting us to the best house. First, we had to overcome all of the layers of fear and resistance. It made me a believer that the bigger the opportunity to lean into massive, crippling fear, the bigger the reward.

While you may be able to argue with Hannah's story, saying she could always move back, you can't argue with my story. We had every excuse in the book to not take this opportunity, let alone find it. The Universe didn't even put the job glaringly in front of Ryan. We had to dig.

That's why I urge my clients—and you, reader—to pay attention and take everything as a sign. It's not a fluke that somebody said something at a restaurant a table away that you heard and resonated with. It's not a fluke that a certain song with certain lyrics came on. It's not a fluke that you're reading this book and hearing these stories. All of these things are the Universe giving you bread crumbs. You just need the guts to follow the clues.

GUIDING LIGHT: OPRAH

I realize this is going to sound white-girl basic, but Oprah was a huge influence on my decision to move. Oprah was a Chicago tried-and-true woman. Then, seemingly out of the blue, she said (not in these exact words), "Fuck it, I'm out. I'm going to Montecito. I need to see the sun."

Everyone was dumbfounded. She was the epitome of Midwest pride. She was unofficial royalty in Chicago. When she left, I realized that I was never going to win an award for enduring the worst winters on record. I didn't have to keep living in the Midwest forever because that's where my parents and their parents and their parents decided we should live.

I could leave.

I also had an unofficial Guiding Light that helped guide me too—a Guiding Light walking among us, if you will.

When I worked for **vitamin**water, I was at a national meeting in Texas and ended up sitting next to Mark Balok, our West Coast Vice President, in one of the shuttles we were taking to dinner. To pass the time, he asked me about Chicago. It was February, so the weather in Chicago was brutal and I told him as much.

He was living In Southern California at the time and said, "You know, you don't have to live like that. There's a better way. It's paradise where I live every single day. You could live there too."

My mind was blown. It was as if he was telling me to follow him to the promised land. He gave me permission to let my mind consider: "What if we did move there?"

Six years later, before I had manifested the move, I messaged him on LinkedIn: *Hi, Mark. I'm finally going to take your advice. We're going to move to California.* He sent me a wonderful message back, and he even helped us scout what cities in SoCal were best for families.

While most of the Guiding Lights I talk about in this book are bestselling authors, your Guiding Light doesn't have to be famous or world renowned. There are messengers out there for you—people who said something off-hand that resonated and that you remember for years. Those are your Spirit guides. It's okay to lean into those conversations and take them as messages from your nonphysical self.

When I told him we wanted to go to NorCal, he asked me what I was thinking. "You're going from bad weather to slightly better bad weather." I didn't want to listen, but eventually I did and was rewarded. Sometimes you have to be willing to rewrite the plan by listening to these guides that reveal themselves.

LET GO OR BE DRAGGED

GIVE UP THE FIGHT TO EXPAND AND GROW

"I got fucking fired."

—NIKKI

MEET NIKKI

Nikki worked at a large Fortune 500 company for nine years. After three failed rounds of IVF, she finally got pregnant. When she reached out to me, she was on maternity leave and was going back into the office in about a month. She wanted support around reentry and navigating the demands of her job with her new child. She was understandably nervous about going back, because while she was on maternity leave, she was demoted from senior director to director. They gave her prematernity position to a woman who was single without kids.

Yeah, I know. I can feel you groaning as you read this.

They tried to play it off like it was a lateral move, but they knew, and Nikki knew, it wasn't—they even took away several people she was managing. She knew returning to work would take grace, finesse, and negotiating boundaries. She wanted to make sure that she was managing her expectations, but be able to push back if they tried to chip away at her responsibilities.

As soon as she went back, it was clear that she was being punished for daring to have a child. She was left off calls and wasn't invited to critical meetings. She had been demoted, and she was no longer on a fast track for career growth within that organization.

To add to the pressure, the company hired a new CEO who was the type to "freshen up" the existing team members upon arrival (i.e., fire the existing team and replace them with his own people). Plus, she was commuting forty-five minutes each way by train. That was at least an hour and a half a day that could have been precious time spent with her new baby she had fought so hard to have. She requested to work from home at least one day a week so that she could see her baby boy before he went to bed at night, but they kept denying her.

Here Nikki is: back in the office, doing the same amount of work with way more bullshit to put up with, less responsibility, title change, and going through awful postpartum because her son is three months old and she's leaving him with a nanny all day, five days a week.

I said to Nikki, "I think we need to look at another opportunity. Why don't we just get you out of there?" A question I often ask my clients is, "Is your job salvageable?" Nikki was really unsure. She told me, "I don't know, but I've been here so long and everybody knows me." It felt safe to her. However, I was trying to get her to see that it wasn't safe anymore. They were starting to take advantage of her because she was loyal to a fault.

Over the next three months, the situation continued to deteriorate. She was having frequent confrontations with her boss. Executive leadership was publicly embarrassing her in meetings, trying to blame her for issues that weren't her responsibility anymore. (It was this new person who had taken her job's responsibility.) On one of our calls, she was in a phone booth at the office, and she started crying, saying, "I hate it here. I hate it." I told her, "Then let's get the fuck out. You can leave. You do not need to stay there." However, she was a glutton for punishment. She would not leave. We ended our time together, during which we set her up with a solid LinkedIn profile and résumé, but at the time, she was not ready to let go.

Then, about two months later, she texted me: "They fucking fired me." I called her, secretly ecstatic while she was screaming. She was irate. She was yelling, "Oh my God, can you fucking believe this?" I told her, "Nikki, the Universe is forcing you out because it's saying this is not good enough for you. Because you couldn't see it on your own, it is forcing you to see it."

The Universe was putting up a "road closed" sign for Nikki after it had repeatedly said, merge, merge, merge, merge, merge.

Anybody who's been fired has likely felt the way Nikki did, but it's always a blessing. Nikki, however, became mired in the anger around it. She felt betrayed. She started talking about suing them for wrongful termination after maternity leave. We did explore that (because, honestly, she had a case), but for Nikki's mental and emotional health, that was not the best course of action. It would have dragged the situation on for much longer, kept her at a low vibration and away from getting the next thing. She stayed angry for a solid four months, and during those months, we paused our work together because she wasn't ready to move on.

Finally, she reached out to start working together again. She had worked through the anger and was ready to move forward. But for those four long months, she was unemployed and at home, stewing in her rage, feeling humiliated. If only she had been able to let go when they first started to mess with her, she would never have been in this position of anger.

This is where the dragging part of "let go or be dragged" comes in. She was dragged for the three months she was back after maternity leave, and then dragged for another four months after that. All because she refused to close the door with gratitude and say, "You know what? I'm going to trust that this firing, even though it really hurts, was for the best." She was unable to see the light at the end of the tunnel.

When she told me she was fired, I told her it was a gift. She (strongly) disagreed. But when you looked at her situation, it truly was. She had a spouse who was making money. She was given four months of severance. There was no reason to panic. I tried to remind her that she hated the job. I told her, "You said at the beginning of every call that you hated it there and you hated the commute. You cried in the pods on our calls. You were getting angry and holding onto a job that you didn't love anymore."

Sometimes the Universe will push us. It will say, "You know what? You no longer have control over this. I've given you the opportunities. If you're not going to do it, I will do it for you." That is the love and awesomeness of the Universe. It will make the decision for you if you can't figure it out.

GUIDING LIGHT: DAVID HAWKINS

"Behind all of the 'I can'ts' are merely 'I won'ts.' The 'I won'ts' mean 'I am afraid to' or 'I am ashamed to' or 'I have too much pride to try, for fear I might fail.' Behind that is anger at ourselves and circumstances engendered by pride."

—DAVID HAWKINS

David Hawkins is an incredible PhD who wrote a book about why we hold onto things titled *Letting Go*. One of my favorite quotes from the book is, "Behind all of the 'I cant's' are merely 'I wont's.'" Saying "I can't" is a big opportunity for us to examine *why* we're driven to do or not do certain things. Once we understand what's hindering us from accepting or embracing change, we can let go of those feelings so we can move forward. Acknowledging and letting go of these feelings allow us to rise up to courage and, with that, finally acceptance and an inner peacefulness.

He is also on the forefront of muscle testing. Muscle testing is another tool that you can use to listen to your Soul. With much practice and training it can give you physical confirmation or denial about something you're thinking about by asking your body. It's this idea that there is a physical memory system that can override your subconscious mind.

I took a course on muscle testing, and learned to use my fingers to muscle test. For instance, I'll ask a yes or no question and depending on how my overlapped fingers move, I'll get an answer that's not really coming from my brain. It's coming from my physical body. People often use it when they are deciding what vitamins to take. They'll ask their body, then stand in a specific pose with their arms crossed over their chest, and their body will lean forward for yes and backward for no. It can take some practice before you can fully trust it, but once confident, it's a great way to get in tune with your subconscious.

If you get confirmation from your body that something is a good idea, it's a lot easier for you to then move forward. It gives you validation. You have all the answers. You just need to learn the ways to listen to yourself.

SPIRITUAL STEPS

I had Nikki, my skeptical New Yorker, use a focus wheel. (If she can use a focus wheel, anyone can use a focus wheel.)

To make a focus wheel, take a piece of paper and draw a small circle in the middle. Then, create twelve lines out from the circle to create twelve "pie slices." Think *Wheel of Fortune*. (I have a template on the app for you to download which will help.)

THE FOCUS WHEEL PROCESS

Ask and It Is Given, by Esther and Jerry Hicks

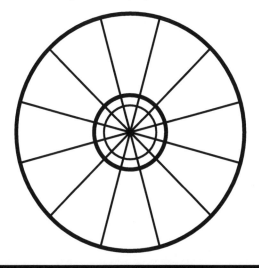

INSTRUCTIONS

1. Make a list of things you DON'T want.
2. Based on that list, create a list of things you DO want. Pick one main thing or feeling all of your desires center around.
3. Write it in the center of the wheel.
4. Imagine the wheel as it is spinning at the vibration of your desire.
5. Think of a statement about the desire.

6. Find statements that feel less resistant until one resonates with your desire.

7. Write that statement at the twelve o'clock position.

8. Ride that wave and continue writing statements in the eleven remaining sections.

9. Write a statement from where you are now vibrationally in the outer-middle circle.

EXAMPLES

"I don't want to stress about money."

"I want to make more money so I will feel abundant and free."

"I want to make $1,000,000 this year."
(You don't truly believe it could happen.)

"I've known a lot of people with fewer opportunities and less support than me that have made millions, so I know it's possible."

"I have massive earning potential. I've earned large raises in the past, and I can do it again."

"I know how to network, and I can call in some favors to help me see what else is out there for me. People want to help."

"I feel empowered, and I know I can manifest anything I want in this life!"

In the center, write something that you want to attract into your life. A great example is people who want to get healthier physically. In the center circle, they would write, "I want to feel physically and mentally strong." Then on all these little "slices" around it, they write things that feel good but aren't totally out of the realm of possibility.

You could write, "I want to wake up every day and cleanse my body with a cup of hot water and lemon." What you wouldn't put in that spot is, "I want to lose thirty pounds in one week." Anything that's too far flung, that your mind can't really wrap itself around or fully believe in, flings you off the wheel. It gets it going too fast and you can't stay on, like the metal roundabouts we played on as kids and tried to get fast enough to fling our friends off.

You can create and use multiple focus wheels at the same time. The center of one could be, "I want to get a new job," and another could be, "I want to become a better meditator." For the meditator one, you would write, "I want to feel connected to my Soul through meditation." Then, as you're filling in these other little pieces, they get stronger. It starts with, "I want to carve out thirty seconds each day to count my breath." Then, the next one is, "I want to take two to three minutes each day to meditate." It has to be a buildup in your head, one that your brain can actually see happening in order to help manifest it.

You fill out the whole wheel at one time. Then, a few times a day, you read each statement out loud, finishing with the one in the center.

You need to get in the habit of focusing on what you do want.

Focus wheels give you these little bread crumbs on how to get there. With the focus wheel, the energy around it will get stronger as you complete the circle. When you start to direct and have a laser focus on an outcome, it speeds up the manifestation. I have clients who have filled out thirteen focus wheels at a time, hung them on their walls, and within a short time, will tell me, "Just threw away another two focus wheels 'cause I manifested that shit."

These wheels can be used for anything, big or little. If you've struggled with addictions in any way, it's good to put overcoming them in the focus wheel. If you want to manifest a new job, be sure to include what kind of job, how much you want to make at it, and how that new job will make you feel.

Focus wheels are also great for trying to find friends or romantic partners. Include in it the kinds of people you want to attract in your life. The center circle for a friend could be, "I have somebody whom I feel energetically and spiritually connected to living in California" or "I have somebody to go on walks with and whom I can call if my kid needs to be picked up from school." For a relationship you could write, "I want somebody who wants to have kids." What you don't want to write is, "I want somebody who's seven feet tall and a billionaire." That's going to fling you off the wheel. It has to be things that are realistically possible, even if they feel like a stretch from where you are right now.

You could want to manifest an amazing boss. Write "I want some-body who really values my work, who I have one-on-ones with every week, and who leaves me happy when I get off the call." I've had clients with bosses they weren't meshing well with and when they projected positive energy and sent focus to that relationship, it transformed. That person has to either meet you at your new vibrational level or fall away, and so many times, the bosses raised their vibration as well because my client was coming to them with a different energy.

A really cool thing? You can do this with your kids. Any of the exercises in this book your kids can do with you. It opens a world to them where they believe they could have anything they want, even if it's a new bike or a new best friend or the teacher they want for fourth grade.

Nikki used her focus wheel to be at peace while going through IVF to have a second child. Her wheel helped her see the opportunities that would come whether she had another child or not.

PROFESSIONAL STEPS

Nikki pulled a Costanza.

If you've never watched *Seinfeld*, there's an episode where Jerry's anxious friend George Costanza says that he's been eating tuna on toast every day for the last ten years, and tuna on toast has done nothing for him. He decides he's going to do something different. He's going to do the opposite of everything he thinks is right for him: he's going to have egg salad on rye. When he orders it, this beautiful woman turns around and says that's exactly what she ordered. He walks up to her and says, "I'm George, I'm unemployed, and I live with my parents," and she invites him to sit down.

"Pulling a Costanza" means to do the opposite of the habits you are currently doing.

For Nikki, she thought she needed to get another job in New

York, which meant another long train ride commute. Instead, we talked about flipping the script. Maybe she needed something where she worked 100 percent remote for a small startup, instead of a big company with a lot of red tape and politics. Maybe she needed to look for something in marketing strategy instead of operations. Essentially, we looked at everything with opposite glasses on. How could she do something slightly different than what she'd been doing before?

She needed to learn to loosen her iron grip of control on things she could not control, no matter how much she wanted to. She had the urge to blame everyone when things didn't go the way she tried to force them to go. Instead, she focused on what she could control, such as working out every day and being present with her son.

Making the decision to do things differently opens up a wonderful portal for new things to flow to you. First, though, you have to be able to overcome the thought pattern your brain provides you every day. Start small. If you go on a walk around the same loop, try walking the loop the opposite direction. Or you can get in your car and find another subdivision or park to walk around. Instead of eating at the same restaurant you eat at every Friday night, eat somewhere new.

Habits are good when they're healthy. However, if you get into the habit of doing something just because it feels safe and comfortable and that's what you always do, then when something "bad" happens, it will be harder to see it as a blessing. If you're constantly switching things up, however, you lose your fear of change. Then, if big change is forced upon you, you can see it as something different, not something bad.

Refer back to your habit tracker and take note of what events are leaving you drained or aren't putting you on the path toward your goals—then do the opposite. If you usually wake up and take a twenty-minute walk, instead spend those twenty minutes reading on the couch or riding a bike or talking to a friend. Routines are great, but sometimes you need to blow them up and build a completely new routine doing new things.

NIKKI TODAY

Once she let go of her anger, she started interviewing, and within a month, Nikki landed a job that allowed her to work from home. It was for a smaller startup where she had much more responsibility. This new role gave her the ability to drive the strategy of the company, which was something she used to love about her old job and that had been slowly stripped away from her.

When events that we label as "misfortune" or feeling "wronged" happen, we need to use it as an opportunity to change our perspective. For Nikki, her event was obviously being fired. If she could have seen it as the Universe making the decision for her so something better could come, it would have saved her months of suffering. Every time there's a storm around us, we should see it as a step toward a new chapter where something better can come to us. It's a perspective that can help us let go a lot sooner.

EXPLORE FOR YOURSELF: PULL A COSTANZA

Look at your routines and consider if they are healthy or not healthy. Ask yourself, "Is this empowering me to get to my big goals?" If not, it's time to change your routine. Even if it is, it's still a good opportunity to look at where you can make small changes.

That way, it won't be so scary when you have the opportunity to let go of something.

It can be as simple as looking at what you're cooking for dinner. There are plenty of wonderful subscription services that give you ideas for new meals to prepare every week or month. You can also try making new friends. New people are a wonderful way to get exposure to new places and things you've never thought to try before.

Take a class or go to an event by yourself. I love to go to concerts by myself. I make friends with all the people in my row, and it gets me out of my bubble. It also forces me to figure things out for myself, like where the hell my Uber is after the concert (never easy). Sometimes it doesn't go according to plan, and that's great. It helps me pivot and be open to meeting new people and experiencing new things.

Pick a day and do everything the opposite of what you normally do. This is an easy way to push the limits of your safety zone because you don't have to think hard about how to change things up—you literally just do the opposite. Take a different route to work. Try the independent café on the other side of town.

Whatever you choose to do, the key is to get used to change. The more comfortable you are with change, the easier it is to let go and avoid being dragged.

WHAT'S THE HARM?

What's the harm in letting go of the stuff that hurts?

YEAH, BUT

HOW TO REGAIN YOUR POWER
BY ELIMINATING EXCUSES

"I am constantly at war with myself over what is best for my family income-wise versus what's best for us with regard to Mama's happiness/sanity. I'm spinning my wheels, wasting valuable time, and losing confidence all the while..."

—ANNA

"I feel totally and utterly trapped."

—CINDY

MEET ANNA AND CINDY

Anna lives in Chicago and is a stay-at-home mom with two children under five. She was gifted coaching sessions with me and sometimes, when coaching is a gift, people don't get great results. One, because it's not their money on the line, and two, it wasn't necessarily their decision to do it.

When I talked to her, she told me she was nervous because she felt pressure to get incredible results. I said, "This is about you, your journey, and feeling better about yourself, not some arbitrary results you have in your head." She reluctantly came on.

Anna had been a lawyer before she married and had kids. However, she never loved it or had passion for the law. She was just doing it because it was a "good and safe" job, and I had a hunch she wanted to make her parents proud.

I get so many lawyer clients, and I always kind of wonder about the root of why they chose that profession. Is it a profession they chose to make their parents proud? Is it a profession they chose because they knew it would give them some sort of inherent status in society? Is it really because they love the law? I've found that the last one is rarely the case.

Let's set the stage for Anna. She was living in Chicago, and her husband was a lawyer. On the first call, she told me that her marriage was incredibly strained because they had made a "deal" that she would go back to work a year after their second child had been born. At the time, her kids were two and four, so she was feeling a lot of pressure from her husband to start being a financial contributor again. However, while she didn't want to go back to law, she *also* didn't really want to be a stay-at-home mom any longer. This was the problem we needed to solve.

As we got into the work, she started to have more intense disagreements with her husband. It got to the point where she hinted that if she didn't figure this out, there was a potential for divorce. Imagine the kind of pressure on this woman. Unfortunately, while there are transferable skills that come with a law degree, there's not always an obvious alternative career path. Plus, she had made such huge financial investments in becoming a lawyer that walking away felt like a waste.

I asked her if there was any way she could write or legally consult for other companies, and she had a visceral negative reaction to going back to the law. She wanted nothing to do with it. Since we were starting at ground zero, I asked her what she enjoyed doing. She replied, "I love to write, and I love to create art." She showed me the napkins she puts in her kids' lunch boxes. On them, she draws amazing pictures. I'm telling you, these napkins are frameable. I told her, "There are all of these wonderful mommy blogs. What if you start guest writing for some of them and posting your art? Then you can start getting paid for that, and maybe start your own."

She initially lit up at the idea, but it seemed like too big a mountain for her to climb. Instead, she thought she needed to start making money right away, and blogging would take too long to monetize. Her husband, she said, would be breathing down her neck the entire time.

Anna had a *lot* of excuses.

Every time we'd have a call, I would ask, "How did the writing go?" She'd say, "Oh, I didn't get to it because of the kids." In reality, there was time to do it, but she had deprioritized herself for so long that carving out time to do something just for herself was scary. She used her kids as the ultimate excuse, yet she was in denial that she was giving excuses. For her, they were legitimate: "The kids didn't take a nap today, so I wasn't able to do anything all week."

As a mom, I get it. Sometimes days don't go the way we planned. However, we would go months between sessions. It got to the point that every time I saw we had a session in the calendar, I knew I was going to get an "I need to reschedule." email. She had too much resistance.

Then there's Cindy. Cindy used excuses in a different way: blame.

Cindy had worked at the same company for over ten years, and she kept getting looked over. She wasn't getting promoted. She felt stuck. Where she lived in the far Northeast, there were few options, and her current company was the only game in town, unless she wanted a long commute to the nearest large city.

She was unhappy at her job, and she was estranged from most of her family in the area. She had a husband who was unemployed and drunk every night. They were basically roommates at that point, but she wouldn't divorce the husband because they have a twelve-year-old son.

After hearing her story, I told her she needed to get the hell out of there.

She refused. Instead, Cindy blamed everyone else. She blamed her company for not acknowledging her genius. She blamed her husband for not handling his addiction. She was one of the most disempowered people I've ever worked with because she had so much blame for everybody but herself.

She believed that if everybody *else* would change, then she would be able to do what she wanted. If only her company would see all this extra effort she was putting in and give her everything she wanted, she wouldn't have to leave. She was even low-key blaming her son. She assumed he wouldn't want to move to a new school, so she used him as an excuse for being unable to relocate to a bigger city with more opportunities.

We talked through her options. She even interviewed with companies that wanted to hire her, but because this was pre-pandemic, she would have had to move. She refused, but not because she couldn't afford it. Her excuse was her son. I wanted to know, "Have you asked *him* if he's willing to move?" She said, "God, no, because I *know* he's not." She wouldn't even ask.

She was blaming everyone around her for her massive amount of unhappiness, but at the same time, she wasn't willing to do anything to change it.

Eventually, she started to blame me: "You should be helping me more. You should be getting me a job." I made it very clear to her I'm not a temp agency and that was not our agreement. We were working together to get to the bottom of this mindset so that she could go further. However, she was so focused on everybody else, and what she felt like they were doing to her, that she couldn't look inward. She was too scared to examine the part that she was playing, which was everything.

I love the saying, "It's never them. It's always you."

Whenever there's negativity coming at you, it's not about you. It's their shit that they're projecting on you. When you're spewing negativity and blaming everybody else—which Cindy was—it's not them, it's *you*. Cindy's blame was from childhood trauma and abuse that had never been dealt with. Nobody protected her.

Nobody looked out for her. So you can see how she could start blaming other people at a very young age. That became how she dealt with things. When something happens in your life that you don't feel is fair or you feel you're being mistreated, it's easy to blame others versus advocating for yourself.

However, let's be very clear here: no child is EVER at fault for being abused. Of course I'm not saying anything like that. I'm saying that trauma caused this behavior later on where she felt powerless, and powerless people blame others for everything. She needed to learn how to take her power back.

GUIDING LIGHT: WAYNE DYER

I wish I had been able to meet Wayne Dyer in person. He, like all of our Guiding Lights, was incredible. He beautifully calls bullshit on excuses.

If you're skeptical of this spirituality "stuff," start with Wayne and his book *Excuses Begone!* He will call you on your shit immediately. Then, you can go deeper and have more results and expansion. I always have clients start with Wayne. He's the least "woo" of all our Guiding Lights. He was a licensed psychologist and extremely credible in his field.

Wayne eloquently explains the relationship between disempowerment and excuses. When you hide behind excuses, therefore blaming others, you disempower yourself. You give others all of your power. "You did this to me. You made me this way, and because of this pain, I can't do anything." That's the excuse. When you start taking 100 percent responsibility, you take your power back.

Think about the last time you were around someone who was giving excuses or blaming others. Didn't you immediately see them as weak? When I listen to someone give excuses, I don't think, "Oh, that other person is a dick." I think, "Wow. I have compassion for you because you're speaking from a disempowered place."

Using excuses makes you come off as weak, especially professionally. You cannot be in any high-level executive leadership position and hide behind excuses. Your board of directors doesn't care what the extenuating circumstances were for that quarter. You had a number to hit.

At the end of the day, you have to embrace the mantra "the buck stops with me" for everything. That is where you find your power. Until you start to take ownership and accountability, you will never have the power to create or manifest the things that you want in your life.

Life is always better when you don't give an excuse. People love it when you say, "You know what, I fucked up." Those three words are magic: "I fucked up." That's all you have to say. When my husband does something and he starts giving excuses, I interrupt to say, "Just say you fucked up, and we're good." Everyone messes up at some point. Admit it, apologize, and try not to do it again.

However, don't wait for an apology to come to you. You need to get to a place where you don't need an apology. There are people who say, "I was domestically abused for ten years. How is that my fault? How is that an excuse?" I think that there are lots of extenuating circumstances, but you have to honor your part in it and say, "I allowed that to happen for a very long time. I messed up." Many of the women I've talked to in those situations admit that they allowed it to happen, and they should have left earlier.

There's power in claiming a situation as yours, because then it's, "I made a choice," instead of, "This person controlled me." It's "I made a choice to stay in that. I made a choice to start dating that person to begin with. I made a choice to have children with that person." The boss thing to do is to own it as a decision *you* made. People respect you because when you own it, you model to your children, your employees, and your family how to claim their own excuses.

When somebody is laying blame on you or somebody else, it's easy to tell that they are trying to get out of their own accountability. It can either reinforce your opinion of them in a negative light or make your opinion worse because what they're doing is fully transparent. No one is fooled by excuses.

SPIRITUAL STEPS

Go on a brain detox. Maybe you watch the evening news or follow toxic influencers. All of these things are fine in the normal course of your life, but when you are trying to make a drastic change in your life for the better, you need to edit out anything that doesn't make you feel good after interacting with it.

Not making you feel *bad* isn't enough. Indifference has to go.

Go on a brain diet. You don't have to give up social media completely—there's a lot of great content out there. If there's a feed that makes you belly laugh every time you see it, keep following that. You don't need to *just* consume motivational inspirational stuff. But if there's a friend or celebrity that always makes you feel stupid or ugly or anything no good, mute them. If it's a friend, you don't have to ghost them. Take the same approach as you do with your Negative Nancy aunt and tell them you'll be unavailable for a while.

Make sure that the stuff you're consuming, whether it be TV shows or social media, isn't going to amplify Debbie Downer's voice. Consume media that is in alignment with your Soul and pushes you out of your comfort zone. **Don't feed the wrong voice.**

PROFESSIONAL STEPS

Both of these women bailed halfway through their professional steps. They are prime examples of strong tigers too afraid to leave the cage. They took a few steps onto the grass, saw that everything was different and there would be a lot of change, and stepped right back behind the bars.

Both of them said they were committed to starting a new job or career path. But halfway through what they needed to do to manifest what they wanted, they stopped. They quit on themselves. They quit coming to calls. They retreated back into their uncomfortable comfort zone.

They wanted someone to pull them out of the ditch instead of doing the work themselves. People can help you, they can reach out an arm, but no one will ever be able to pull you out of the hole you are in without you taking action.

Anna and Cindy both refused to truly commit. If there's something in your life that you want to change, whether it's finding a new relationship, getting a new job, or making new friends, you have to commit to it and treat it like a job. You have to find time for it. Put it on your calendar; have people hold you accountable.

ANNA AND CINDY TODAY

This chapter is in part a cautionary tale about not being able to see all the hands that are trying to help you out of the hole.

But I'm so glad to report that Anna has started to step out of the cage. She's still a stay-at-home mom, but since the pandemic, she has leaned into her art. She even exhibited her drawings at a local craft fair, which was a huge step. Her husband was supportive and didn't let her back out in the ninth hour. Her daughters, albeit confused, saw their mom put her own interest first. What a gift to give them!

She has greatness living inside her: she went to law school, she passed the bar, and she is a gifted artist—and she's starting to see that reflection in the mirror. Even though she was gradually sliding into mediocrity and misalignment, she's deciding to fight back and resist being swallowed by excuses and denial. The ideologies that we talked about—Spirits of alignment and having faith in yourself—I want to hope that some of those got through to her, and judging by her recent accomplishments, they have.

Cindy, on the other hand, is still in the same small town, stuck in her unfulfilling job, in a marriage she hates, and surrounded by a family she feels betrayed her.

All of the chapters so far have had clients' stories that show incredible results, but it doesn't always work out that way. If you don't use the tools and put in the work, you won't have results.

A NOTE ON STAY-AT-HOME MOMS

I have no interest in insulting stay-at-home moms, but I do want to blow the whistle. If you don't want to be a stay-at-home mom anymore, but you've had a long gap in your résumé, don't use that as an excuse. With stay-at-home moms especially, kids are a beautiful excuse to stay stuck.

Don't get me wrong; sometimes it's a legitimate excuse. However, at the end of the day, you're going to end up resenting your children if they're the reason you don't have professional fulfillment. It also causes a power imbalance in your marriage. How much power is being a SAHM giving your spouse? Financial power is power in the relationship. Period. If you have to ask your husband to spend money, not only does it not look good, but it probably doesn't feel good either.

There are some women who truly thrive as stay-at-home moms: the ones who grew up knowing that was what they wanted to do, and they love it. However, that's not true for most women. Being a SAHM becomes a label that you can hide behind, pretending that it's pride. "I take pride in being a stay-at-home mom." Absolutely you can, but you also likely felt a lot of pride and fulfillment when you were working.

However, stay-at-home mom pride is not the same as professional success pride. They are two different things, and sometimes you need to switch in and out of them. To stay stuck in the stay-at-home mom space can be a status quo trap and feel very disempowering. There are so many stay-at-home moms who do not want to be or did not choose that path, and now they're scared to say they don't want to do it anymore. Don't be that person. I see so many women walking around as shells of themselves, and no one wants that for you—especially your kids.

A big reason women are scared to say that they don't want to be SAHMs is because of the backlash from the sorority of other stay-at-home moms. Instead, you need to tap into yourself, get back in alignment, and figure out what you want long-term. Unfog that mirror.

If your goal is living for your kids, that might be problematic later. What will you do when the kids leave? The whole point is to eventually have them leave the house. From day one, you're teaching them how to exist on their own. If you've been using them as an excuse their whole lives, you'll end up saying, "Well, I was taking care of you or I would've started that business thing or I would have done XYZ." That's unfair to you *and* unfair to your children.

I want you to truly look and see how much you're using your kids as an excuse to hide behind. Don't fall for the idea that it's easier to stay where you are (miserable) and accept this is what your life is going to be. You are never too far gone from the workforce to get back in. You should at least *try* to go back to work if you feel called to. Going back can take many forms: a part-time on-site job, a remote gig, or an entrepreneurial venture.

Then, if you feel like it's not a fit and you'd rather be a stay-at-home mom, great. Now you won't have any resentment because you tried. But to stay indefinitely out of the workforce after your kids are born keeps you blind to all of the other pleasures and joys you could get throughout your day.

EXPLORE FOR YOURSELF: OWN YOUR SHIT

Identify and evaluate the stories you are telling yourself. Realize all of the disempowering thoughts that you've linked with your "identity." Who are you letting chip away at the power you inherently have? By proactively blaming them and by not taking accountability, you're letting them steal your power without a fight.

Look at situations where you're trash talking or spewing negativity. Then turn the mirror around and realize that it's not them. It's *you*. You are the one holding onto this story. You are choosing to be in a relationship that is toxic, whether it's with a company or a partner.

Repeat after me: It's not them. It's you. It's always you. It always has been you, and it always will be you. Remember, the source of the negativity is the problem, not the receiver. We have to stop blaming our parents or our children or our spouses. Take accountability and take action.

You should also evaluate the excuses you tell yourself every day. Every time you catch yourself making an excuse, write it down and put it in a jar. Challenge your family, friends, or roommates to help keep you honest. It's a great way to physically see how many excuses you give in a day, week, or month. If you need a physical accountability method, keep a hairband around your wrist and snap it every time you give an excuse.

Get really comfortable with owning those three magic words "I fucked up" and see what happens.

If you are a visual person, grab a piece of paper and make two columns. On the left side, write a list of things you want to do. On the right side, write why you are not doing them. Then, go through and label each of those reasons as an excuse—because that's what they are.

WHAT'S THE HARM?

What's the harm in reclaiming your power by taking accountability for *everything*?

MOVE THE MOPED

CUT ENERGETIC TIES TO ANYTHING MEDIOCRE

"I feel like such an idiot. I always make the wrong choices."

—SHANNON

MEET SHANNON

Shannon was in her mid-forties and had worked for the biggest brands in cosmetics. She left one of the largest brands to go to a startup beauty company. Unfortunately, within two years, the brand didn't go viral and she got blamed as the SVP of Sales and Marketing.

When she came to me, she believed she had aged out of the industry. It's an industry where everyone talks, reputations get around, and she felt like they had put her to the curb. She questioned her own competence and talent. She wanted help finding a new job, but at the same time, she believed she'd have to trick somebody into hiring her because her confidence was so low.

Through our work together, Shannon admitted that she wanted to start her own beauty brand. However, she had a lot of doubts. She thought there was no way it could happen, because her negative beliefs were telling her why she couldn't do it. I told her, "We need to create space for something to manifest. You don't have to figure it out. Instead, you need to get off the negative talk track, and spend some time being okay with this chapter being closed and waiting for the next thing to come. The next thing, however, needs to be something where you're doing your own brand."

However, there was something blocking Shannon's manifestation. You can't manifest what you want if there is something else holding that energetic space. Imagine you have one parking spot, and there's an ugly, beat-up moped in the middle of it. You think that another car could fit in—you think that what you want to manifest can get in—but it can't until you move that moped out of the space. You need to clear the bad energy out of your Spirit before your manifestation can move in.

Shannon's "moped" was working for other people. She thought she needed to be a CEO somewhere else first, then start her own thing. I pushed back and said, "No, because you want to do it right now. The Universe clearly pushed you out of this job so that you could make room to create your own brand."

GUIDING LIGHT: ESTHER HICKS

"Every thought vibrates, every thought radiates a signal and attracts a matching signal back. The only reason that you could ever experience something other than what you desire is because you are giving the majority of your attention to something other than what you desire."

—ESTHER HICKS

Esther Hicks is a channeler for Abraham Hicks. Abraham is the spokesperson for all of the energy collective that isn't of this plane, which some people would call angels. Abraham talks through Esther, and now, she's world renowned. What Abraham teaches through Esther is the idea that what we spend our time focusing on is what we're going to draw in.

Abraham is very accepting of you staying on your negative plane. If you want to, that's no problem. But just know that there's all of this abundance, all of this stuff that you've put in your vortex, that can't find you if you're on that lower vibration. All the things you want to manifest for yourself—a certain car, that perfect partner, that new job—are in your vortex. The moment you think of it or say what you want, it goes into your own, personal wonderful vortex. Nobody else can get things in our vortex because they have their own.

For Shannon, if she wants to have her own beauty brand, nobody else can get to it. It's only hers; it's locked in there. However, until she got her vibrational level to a better place than it was when we started it, the things in her vortex couldn't flow to her.

Esther explains that, if you are feeling a negative emotion, you don't have to get fully positive immediately. All you have to do is reach for an emotion that's slightly higher on the vibrational scale than the emotion you have right now.

EMOTIONAL GUIDANCE SCALE

by Abraham-Hicks

1. Joy/Appreciation/Empowerment/Freedom/Love
2. Passion
3. Enthusiasm/Eagerness/Happiness
4. Positive Expectation/Belief
5. Optimism
6. Hopefulness
7. Contentment
8. Boredom
9. Pessimism
10. Frustration/Irritation/Impatience
11. Overwhelm
12. Disappointment
13. Doubt
14. Worry
15. Blame
16. Discouragement
17. Anger
18. Revenge
19. Hatred/Rage
20. Jealousy
21. Insecurity/Guilt/Unworthiness
22. Fear/Grief/Desperation/Despair/Powerlessness

When I work with clients, I explain that if you're feeling jealous, that's okay. We just want to reach for one emotion above jealousy. We don't have to get all the way up to joy and ecstasy. All we need to do is get to hatred. If you can go from jealousy to hatred or rage, or if you can go from rage to revenge or revenge to anger, you're moving up the scale. The very lowest emotions on this scale are fear, grief, depression, and apathy. You don't have to get from those to the very top, which are joy, empowered, freedom, and love. You can just get to disappointment, which is ten rungs higher. Climb the ladder one emotional rung at a time.

Shannon took baby steps to climb the ladder because getting to the top was too steep for one jump. Once you start the climb, good things will start coming, and then you start to feel even better. When you start to see your life change, you can go one rung higher, then five rungs higher. All of the things in your vortex are on the high end of this emotional scale. Once you get up there, those things come to you. The best part is you don't have to worry about somebody else getting it first because it's in *your* vortex. They can't get to it. Your only job is to manage your emotions.

When Shannon was terrified, she would reach for a better feeling, and this was the driver that allowed all of this other stuff to come to her. Feeling like a fraud is still higher on the emotional scale than apathy, which is where she was when we started.

Like Shannon, you just need to climb the ladder one rung at a time to get yourself out of the low point.

SPIRITUAL STEPS

Shannon had to focus on energy clearing in order to move the moped, and you do too.

Take physical stock of the main thing you are trying to manifest. This is a great exercise for relationships. Whether you are trying to find new adult friends or you are in a relationship that's no longer serving you, you won't be able to get what you want until you release what is currently holding that space—because they both can't fit at the same time.

For Shannon, the space was filled with the idea that she needed to take a job with another cosmetics company, and then while she was working there, she could have a "side hustle" to start her own beauty brand. However, there was no reason she couldn't start her brand right away. She could afford not to work for a few months. She had the resources and connections to start this dream right away. If she started working at another company, there was no way she would come back to her dream.

She needed to completely purge that thought—move that moped—from her mind. She had to close the door completely. I had to do the same thing when I started my coaching business. There is no way I would have ever started my business if I had taken one of the jobs I applied for when I panicked and listened to resistance.

If you want a new relationship, you have to cut ties with the old relationship. If you don't, you are being drained because you are energetically connected to that person, and no one else can manifest in your life while you're still connected. Clear your moped so you can make room for the Range Rover.

PROFESSIONAL STEPS

After parting ways with her previous employer, Shannon was feeling a lot of imposter syndrome. Before she could start manifesting the next job, she needed to get out of the pool of uncertainty she was swimming in. To counteract that imposter syndrome, we needed to make her a subject matter expert—which she was. Her whole career was in color cosmetics. She *is* the beauty industry. And yet, she was hesitant to write an article on LinkedIn (which you can do for free) or on any other outlet.

Like many women, Shannon was terrified she was going to write something that would come off as dumb or foolish. However, she needed to lean into the fact that she was an expert in this field, and that if she wrote an article about the top three color cosmetic trends she was seeing, it would be her opinion and *that* was valuable.

She started publishing, and while it was terrifying in the beginning, she was able to raise her visibility on LinkedIn. Plus, when people see you have taken the time to write an article about your industry, it's going to position you in a place of credibility. It didn't take long for people to begin reaching out to her, some of whom were people from past companies she'd worked for.

Once they reconnected with her, whether that was via phone call or DMs, I would push her to write them a LinkedIn recommendation. It's a common misconception that you can't write a recommendation unless it's someone you directly work with. That's not true. It can be someone that you had a really good conversation with. Categorize them as someone you know and say things such as *they have great energy or personality*, or *they are a subject matter expert*.

This puts the wheels in motion for the Universe to bring that positive energy back around to you. The more good deeds you put out there, the faster the wheel spins to bring good deeds back to you. But Shannon's intention wasn't to bring good back to her—she just wanted to spread good vibes. The wonderful, surprising results were amazing opportunities that came to her.

The Universe tempted her with an opportunity to work for someone else in a high-level role making a lot of money. It also gave her the opportunity to work with a cosmetic chemist who wanted to start his own brand—and who wanted her to join him. Shannon was scared to join him. It felt risky to her. But when the Universe sends you a lifeline and you don't snatch it, it won't come around again. You have to take the leap before you're ready. She overcame her imposter syndrome, raised her vibration, and took the leap.

SHANNON TODAY

The person who wanted to work with Shannon was a co-founder and chemist behind a major beauty brand, and it was a huge deal. When Shannon told me that he reached out about wanting to start his own beauty brand, and that he wanted to collaborate with her, I was ecstatic. I told her, "Shannon, this is the Range Rover. We got the moped out, and now here's this Range Rover waiting to park. It's got its turn signal on."

Once she started taking meetings with him, she got excited. Then she said, "It's really risky." She started talking about taking any job she could get, and at this point, she probably would have had to take something less than an SVP because she was desperate and you could smell it on her.

I said, "No, this is it. This is the Universe bringing you something new, and you don't even have to come up with all the money. This is the money guy. He's got all these investors, yet you get to be the co-founder of this brand. I don't see a downside." However, Shannon had let that external criticism get into her brain so deeply that even when something shiny and perfect for her was in front of her, it was difficult for her to believe it and grasp it.

However, thanks to the work we did together, Shannon was able to step out of her cage and co-found an amazing new beauty brand. Her dream of creating a company that's not just about the product but about the people who work there has become a reality—and that was born from her being cast to the side. None of this would have happened if she hadn't been let go.

She went from someone who was counting the years until she could retire to co-founder and owner of a major beauty brand. She's proud and happy that her employees want to work there, because they feel seen and valued.

EXPLORE FOR YOURSELF: GET WITCHY

I send all of my clients an oracle deck when we first start working together—even the most skeptical ones—and I tell them whenever they need immediate guidance, instead of waiting for an angel sign, to use the deck.

I've provided a link to the oracle deck I recommend in the Resources section, but you can use whatever deck calls out to you.

Any time they have a question they are stuck on, I remind them to ask the deck. "Do I ask for more money?" Ask the deck. "Do I move into this new career?" Ask the deck. Look for "jumpers"—cards that fall to the side or "jump" while shuffling rapidly. You can also randomly pull cards and whichever ones resonate with you, are meant for you. In fact, every client that has asked a question of the deck has gotten an answer that is very specific to them and their fears around that situation.

Shannon used her oracle deck while deciding whether to start her new brand. And remember Nikki, our skeptical New Yorker? She never used the oracle deck while we were working together. But recently, I received a text from her:

I was looking for a pen in my desk drawer and saw the oracle deck. So I decided to give it a flip through and a card fell right out.

The card was the New Beginnings card: "Everything in life is constantly vibrating and moving, and therefore, continuously changing and evolving. Be aware that a new beginning is on the horizon. Have courage and faith, because right now, life is trying to nudge you forward and move you in a new direction."

I was ecstatic, because Nikki was currently at a crossroads with her job. "You get that it was not a coincidence that you saw that deck AND pulled that card? Right?" Nikki agreed and admitted that I've rubbed off on her. The card proved to be true. Not long after, Nikki got a new job that felt truly in alignment with her Soul.

WHAT'S THE HARM?

What's the harm in focusing on what feels good?

DEVIL ON MY SHOULDER

ESCAPING MENTAL CONFINEMENT

After a painful breakup my junior year in college, I had my first encounter with bulimia. One of my ex-boyfriend's buddies had mentioned to me that my ex only dated "fat chicks" because they have low self-esteem and he could easily manipulate them. A true gem of a man, right? When I heard that remark it confirmed what my mind had been telling me for years—my weight was the reason I wasn't worthy of love from men. Feeling disgusting and desperate, I overate to feel soothed and comforted, but immediately after, the panic of the consequences would take hold and up it would come.

Fast-forward: ten years later, after I had my first child, Delilah, I experienced peripartum depression, a disorder that affects one in seven mothers[1]. Not feeling like it was an option to deal with my immense anxiety and sadness, I swapped my old coping mechanism, bulimia, for a new one: work.

I diligently returned to my demanding job after twelve weeks of maternity leave on the dot. My management team was composed of men (almost exclusively with stay-at-home wives), so I was back to a road-warrior travel schedule faster than my nether-region stitches could heal.

My first trip took me to Dallas. My male VP of marketing was joining me because we had a buyer meeting with 7-Eleven, a huge national account for us. I walked toward the car rental desk, wearing a semi stretchy dress with layers of Spanx underneath. He saw me, walked up, tapped my lower back/upper booty, and said approvingly, "Wow, you snapped back quick."

I realized that not only was I expected to have a child, but that when she's exactly twelve weeks old, I'd put my still-bleeding, healing body on a plane, create a deck that this douchebag was going to take credit for, and look exactly how I did the last time he saw me at my lowest pre-baby weight.

There was no time to heal. There was no time to rest. I already had high expectations for myself, but I was shocked to hear from a superior that he also had expectations, and his were actually higher than mine.

After that meeting, I went into overdrive. I decided I was going to

1   "What is Peripartum Depression (formerly Postpartum)?" American Psychiatric Association, October, 2020, https://www.psychiatry.org/patients-families/postpartum-depression/what-is-postpartum-depression.

show all of these bros that I could do it all. I was going to come back stronger than I left. They were never even going to hear me talk about my child. I wasn't going to show a picture. It would be as if she didn't exist, because I wanted them to know I was focused 1,000 percent on work. I was willing to do whatever was needed, not to only get back in good standing with them, but to surpass it, even if it meant being less of myself.

So I did. I started filling any free time I had frantically exercising. I put Delilah in the BabyBjörn and went on two to three-mile walks. My goal wasn't to have connection time with her; it was an exercise box that I could check to lessen my thoughts of self-loathing. In hindsight, I wish I had been playing and snuggling with her, rolling around on the floor during tummy time.

There was no additional sleep. There were no massages. There was no yoga. There was work, taking care of Delilah's basic needs, and anything extra I could do to professionally advance.

The only thing that mattered was either moving forward or holding onto some semblance of the reality that I had before giving birth. For a lot of moms, this is when self-care gets totally obliterated. Any bit of self-care we have is the first thing on the list to get crossed out once we have a child—whether you have one or four, it's just gone. That baby's needs, and everybody else's needs, move to the top over yours.

Unsurprisingly, the pressure to "snap back quick" reignited my bulimia. Work trips became my safe place to binge and purge. Purging was a way to physically empty all of the negative energy coming at me both internally and externally. Poison that had built up throughout the days, weeks, and years. It once again became a vicious cycle, because after I purged, the toxic energy came back with a vengeance. Shame would wash over me like a tidal wave: *You're so fucking gross. Why can't you just stop this? What is wrong with you?! Just stop eating!*

Finally, when Delilah was six months old, and I was feeling close to rock bottom, I sought help in the form of a wellness retreat.

When I arrived at Miraval, this wonderful sanctuary of blissed-out guests, practitioners, and healers, I wasn't totally sold that it would "work." To my surprise, the Guiding Lights working there provided me with tons of hope that recovery from my eating disorder was possible. It was a wonderful oasis when I felt so dry and empty, lost in a desert that I couldn't find my way out of.

A lot of people are struggling with this feeling now thanks to a multiyear pandemic and social unrest (and rightfully so). We all thought the wine was going to make us feel good. We all thought being on the couch for eight hours, scrolling our TikTok feed, would feel good. But it didn't. That toxic numbing was only perpetuating the pain that we're feeling and depleting us even more.

While I was at Miraval, I got amazing sleep, ate the cleanest food possible, and embraced the stillness (and lack of crying baby). Miraval was the Soul hug I desperately needed, and it was a total reset. Now, I won't lie and say I didn't have bulimic episodes after that, but they were never the same as before. They were never as intense or as frequent.

So, how did I find my way to healing? Once I was ready, the Universe sent the messenger I needed to drag my ass to Miraval. That's how messengers and teachers show up in your life—randomly.

One night my husband told me, "There's this big fancy party, and this girl, Rachel, who I know from work, is going." I said, "Well, I don't really know her, but okay." After two hours of "going-deep" soul-sister-type conversing, likely sensing I was hanging on by a thread, Rachel invited me on her annual trip to Miraval with her and her best friend, Natalie.

Even though I barely knew them, and the trip was uber pricey, I took the risk and went (and now they're both ride-or-die friends). They were a tandem of love and support right out of the gate that I had never had before. On that trip, I felt safe enough to tell them about my bulimia, a secret I had only shared with Ryan and my therapist. I had known them for a total of three days. Yet, I knew they could help keep me on track and could be a lifeline if I started sliding back to that awful place.

As soon as I told them, Rachel confided she was contemplating getting a divorce. That's the magic—once you start sharing your mess, it gives other people permission to share their mess. On the outside, we were the ones getting the promotions and had the external things that proved we were "successful." On the inside, however, we were all dealing with some tough shit. We had a storm raging in our heads about all the things we needed to do in order to have worth. It felt like the more I produced, the more worth I would have to my boss, to my husband, and to my child.

For me, the result of those mind-storms was a ten-year deterioration of self-worth that intensified with the pregnancy and birth of my first child. To be very clear, it was not her fault. I had zero boundaries around myself and what I deserved as a human. It wasn't even that I put all of my basic needs on the back burner—I let them cease to exist.

A NOTE ON EATING DISORDERS

Do not make the mistake of thinking eating disorders are just for teenagers. Today's eating disorders look different. The control and restriction—whether it's macrobiotic, no sugar, keto, pick your poison—of whole food groups is a warning sign. Addiction to the Peloton, yoga, counting calories: those are potentially problematic disorders.

I see so many women walking around looking like shells of themselves. Decked out in their lulus but not looking strong—in fact, they look emaciated. Are we really going to ignore this? Are we going to pretend this is normal?

Women who take two spin classes a day and then drink a single Bulletproof coffee for their food intake: that's anorexia. Intermittent fasting? When people take it to a whole new level—like waiting to eat until three or four in the afternoon—that sure sounds like anorexia, at least to me. We are out there starving ourselves, and working out on top of it! If we ask ourselves what's the harm in giving yourself what your body wants, the answer might be that it would result in decreased worth. But we couldn't be more wrong.

When we talk about self-care, I want to be extremely clear: *you deserve to eat.* You deserve to sleep. So many women strive to control both of those things. Eating disorders are up 25 to 40 percent today compared to where they were prepandemic.[2]

---

2   William A. Haseltine, "How the Pandemic Is Fueling Eating Disorders in Young People," *Forbes*, December 10, 2021, https://www.forbes.com/sites/williamhaseltine/2021/08/27/how-the-pandemic-is-fueling-eating-disorders-in-young-people/?sh=5a7b51922269.

During quarantine, I gained ten pounds, and it reignited my flame of self-hate—partly because of the extreme stress. My coping mechanism was my eating disorder and that was taken away. Then, when I took away alcohol, it felt like a pressure cooker. All I could think about was how to get relief from this feeling. It was like a stock ticker scrolling constantly in the back of my mind. It had been years since I'd had a slip, but I had multiple slips during the pandemic.

If you struggle like I do, take a hard look at the habits you adopted during the pandemic. It's likely time to make some swaps.

GUIDING LIGHT: MICHAEL SINGER

"Only you can take inner freedom away from yourself, or give it to yourself. Nobody else can."

—MICHAEL SINGER

Are you progressing spiritually, or just strengthening your ego?

Michael introduced me to the idea that you are not your thoughts. Your thoughts are actually a different piece of you. A lot of people call it ego, your monkey mind, or your survival brain. Whatever you want to call it, it's this dueling personality that lives within us and wants us to live in fear all the time. This is the voice that tells you all those negative lies about yourself, because it thinks if it can keep you "on edge," you will be better equipped when the shit inevitably hits the fan. In essence, it tells you all the things you want and don't want—which keep you out of true alignment with your Soul, whose only want is to be okay, to feel good.

Michael explains on his podcast, "You want to feel high. You want to feel well. You want to feel right, and it's so obvious. And it is so simple, but nobody will see that. Nobody will own that. They own all these other things that they want. I want to get married. I want to have a car. I want people to respect me. I want to look better. And there's just millions and billions of things that they say they want. And they also have all these things that they don't want. Eventually you see the wants and the not-wants are the same. Liking and disliking are just different degrees of wanting to be okay."

Michael teaches that that fear-voice isn't us. When these thoughts come up, we need to acknowledge them and then detach from that voice. The voice that tells us we need improvement in some area is *not* your Soul talking. It's the ego. Relax in the face of it. And even though it may get louder, like a child throwing an epic tantrum, it will tire itself and eventually stop because nobody's listening. Then, little by little, the voice will be less frequent and hopefully stop altogether.

Our biggest task in this life is to notice the difference between that ego voice and our Soul's voice.

If you want to go deeper into the subject, Michael's book *The Untethered Soul: The Journey Beyond Yourself* is phenomenal. It does, however, go very deep, which might be too much if you are just dipping your toe in spirituality. This was the first book I ever read on spirituality (because Oprah told me to, and I'm a loyal subject), and it was a little hard for me to wrap my head around. Like most people, I thought my thoughts were me, but Michael is saying those are not you at all. Your feelings are you—the talk track is not.

Even the title of his book is beautiful: *The Untethered Soul.*
Shouldn't that be everybody's ultimate end goal: to feel unbridled
power and alignment with their Soul? There's power and freedom
that comes from detaching from your self-defeating thoughts.
That's how you become untethered: you untether *yourself* from
this voice that is telling you anything that doesn't feel good is
what you deserve.

PRODUCTIVITY DOES NOT EQUAL WORTH

HOW TO GET MORE BY DOING LESS

"Making other people feel good makes me feel good. I only need about three to four hours of sleep each night and I'm okay."

—DR. TINA

"It's a tumor. I have a fucking brain tumor."

—JANE

MEET DR. TINA AND JANE

Initially, Tina sought out working with me because she was trying to garner support for the physicians working at her hospital. She was worried many were on the verge of burnout. However, after we started talking, we decided it was best for her to work with me one-on-one, and if all went to plan, we could expand coaching services to other physicians.

In her very first session I could tell she was in survival mode, but in an exceptionally high-functioning manner. Tina is a friggin' machine. Tina has her shit together. She was sleeping about four to five hours a night. She ate clean. Her office was (and still is) immaculately organized. The one thing in her office that didn't make sense to me was her whiteboard, which had zero white space left. It was overloaded with all the things she was doing. She was writing for different publications, mentoring residents, and taking care of her patients which happened to be teeny tiny, very sick babies.

After our first session, she decided on her goal. She wanted to do more—something in wellness.

Tina had her sight set on becoming her hospital's Chief Wellness Officer. I said, "Oh, okay, so give up being a neonatologist who does rounds or is 'on service' (where you sleep at the hospital and are on call for up to two weeks at a time)?" She said, "No, no, no, no. I mean in *addition* to that." (If only you could have seen my face.) I told her I didn't see how that was possible because she was already working sixty hours a week and has three children, a dog, and a husband. She insisted she could do it, so I asked her, "Tina, what does your self-care look like?"

She explained that she did yoga every once in a while. That was it. Full stop. When we dug into her sleeping habits, she told me that she went to sleep around midnight or one a.m. and woke up around five a.m. However, she was so high functioning that lack of sleep wasn't even something she thought about. In her mind, she just didn't need that much sleep. (False.)

She insisted on going for the Chief Wellness Officer position, so we made a plan. She advocated for herself to her boss, and the hospital sent her to Stanford to attend a weekend workshop with other CWOs around the nation. At the time, there were very few CWOs out there. After the workshop, she brought up the position again to her boss, who said, "Instead of creating that position right away, let's add it to your current responsibilities."

Tina agreed, so, in addition to her current responsibilities, she willingly took on mentoring physicians, discussing physician burnout, and creating a newsletter on wellness. The whiteboard was getting fuller and fuller, and her inbox had over three thousand emails. She asked, "Can you help me get my inbox to zero?" I explained that was not where we needed to start, knowing her underlying goal was to be more organized so that she could free up more space to do more things.

Jane is another client who was teetering on burnout. Not surprisingly she also worked in the healthcare services field, as a psychologist.

When I first met her, I thought, "Am I going to be able to coach a psychologist? Is she going to be resistant to everything that I say?" I'm happy to say, it was the opposite.

When Jane reached out, she felt broken. (I am not a fan of that word, but it is the most accurate.) She was so depleted from the demands of her job that she was hovering on being nonfunctional. She was working fourteen- to sixteen-hour days—burning the candle at both ends.

She was working for an addiction rehabilitation facility, and with over a decade of sobriety under her belt, she was incredibly passionate about her work. She poured all of her time and energy into opening a new rehab facility, because in her mind, the sooner they got the doors open, the sooner they could start helping people.

However, Jane's passion was misaligned with her organization's intention. They, of course, wanted to help people, but there were bottom lines that needed to be met. Jane was often at odds between the helping side of her profession and the business side. When you put together the pressure from her boss and then the internal pressure that she was putting on herself, it was a recipe for burnout.

Jane had also become a little bit addicted to this new job. Although she had over fifteen years of sobriety, she was not immune to other addictions, so the work had become a "healthy addiction." In her company, there were no checks and balances. No one said, "Wait a minute, you're working too long and you're really not focused on your health." Instead, everybody applauded her—like most employers do.

At the end of the day, she was completely exhausted. She wasn't working out. In fact, she wasn't doing anything for herself at all. She was so depleted, she was no longer passionately driven by the greater good that had started her on this path. She was running on fumes, and resentment began to creep in.

She felt angry that she was working so hard but had difficulty setting boundaries. Jane was a pressure cooker, about to blow. We decided the best path was to get her grounded in gratitude exercises so she could change her vibration around work. Everything was going well and she was feeling slight improvement when, in our fourth session, she popped on the Zoom and said,

"I have a fucking brain tumor." I was shocked. She had been having migraines throughout our time working together, but we thought they were just stress-induced. We assumed once she started finding gratitude in her day and taking more time for self-care (she had started running at night and taking spin classes), the migraines would dissipate.

It turns out, the migraines weren't caused by stress.

One day she had a blinding migraine—one that was so bad, she went to the ER. They did a scan and found a brain tumor…and it was hemorrhaging.

GUIDING LIGHT: AMY B. SCHER

Amy Scher (whom I had the pleasure of interviewing on my podcast) had a seven-year battle with Lyme disease, along with a lot of other diagnoses. She did all of the medical recommendations and none of them worked long-term; there was no permanent healing. Instead, she started to look at the treatment of our body from a spiritual health point of view.

Amy teaches us that at the end of the day, it's not only about believing but about taking into action the connection between our physical health and our mental health. In her interview on my podcast, Amy explains, "The body just wants to be heard, just like we all want to be heard. And guess what happens when you don't listen? It screams louder. And your body isn't something you can tell to shut up. If anybody's ever tried that, you'll probably know it does not work at all. The message that I want to get through is let's all take a breather—look at it in a new way, see what it's trying to teach you. You've missed something along the way if you end up in a chronic situation, but that's fine because until it happened you didn't know to pay attention. So it's nothing to beat yourself up about. Things are brewing for a while and we either ignore them or we don't notice them. And once the emotional imbalance sort of takes root in the physical body, then it's like, oh no, now this is kind of a big fix."

She acknowledges that it can be a chicken and egg type scenario. How do you have a good mindset when you feel like shit all day? However, emotional baggage and stress contribute to every imbalance in the mind–body connection.

You store your emotions in different parts of your body (which part is going to be different for everyone), and until you release that baggage, you'll never be able to become the healthiest, happiest version of yourself.

SPIRITUAL STEPS

When Jane told me about her tumor, it was the first time she hadn't complained in one of our sessions. A switch had been flipped. Her attitude was, "Can you believe this shit? I have a fucking brain tumor," instead of weepy hysteria. She was almost casual about it. At first, I thought she was in denial. I had to dig: "What's going on here? Are we not acknowledging what's going on?"

She was fully aware of what was going on—and she had already accepted it. She said, "I'm not surprised, because of course I would manifest this in my body." She knew that she had been driving her body into the ground for years. She believes in the Law of Attraction and physical manifestation (both of which we had worked on in the beginning of her coaching), so at this point, she was in a wonderful mental place. She knew it wasn't a punishment but something that she needed to take accountability for manifesting in her body, herself.

I asked her, "Okay, so what do you think this brain tumor is here to teach you? What do you think we need to do to let it be released from you?" She explained that her doctors were talking about different options, but she decided that rather than "killing it" or "beating it" she'd do the opposite and embrace it.

Instead, I asked, "What if we send it love?" Love for being here, for forcing her to rest and focus on her physical health. We decided she should name it. She immediately said, "Grace." It was the perfect name. It wasn't a negative name. The naming showed the level of acceptance she was already at with the diagnosis.

After that, we checked on Grace in every session. And for a while, I texted her almost every day: *How is Grace doing today? What is Grace telling you today? What can we find as a piece of gratitude for Grace?* During this time, she sent her tumor nothing but good vibes. She did white light meditation. She journaled about why Grace was there.

She became nonresistant to the tumor because she knew that she needed to approach it from a place of love. This was now a piece of her body. If she talked about killing it, she was talking about killing something in her body. Instead, she accepted it to transform it—so she could release it and it could go away. She was constantly sending love and positive energy to Grace.

She never had to do any treatment and continued to get good

news at every follow-up appointment with her doctor…this had all been a fluke and medically she was completely fine. She got really serious about meditation and taking care of herself. She went on a journey of spiritual healing. She took a six-month sabbatical from work. She traveled to five different countries, she rested, she reconnected with herself and her Spirit.

Grace was a wake-up call to be healthy and take a 360-degree approach to her body. It was as important for her mind to be clear and at peace as it was for her body to feel strong.

Six months later, doctors were astounded. Grace has never grown or been a problem since. No migraines. No issues. I want to be clear that Jane never turned down medical advice from her team of professionals. She discussed the best course of action with them and used the above tactics as a way to complement the guidance of her doctors.

With Tina, we started talking about self-care. (This was slightly before the pandemic hit.) She began each day doing yoga with her neighbors, on their front lawns, at seven o'clock in the morning. Next, we tackled sleep—I suggested six hours a night minimum. Her initial reaction was, "Oh my God, I don't think I can do it." But she was willing to give it a try, so a few nights a week, she started sleeping six whole hours. She went from feeling good to feeling amazing and with increased energy and focus.

Tina wasn't trying to fill a depleted cup—she hadn't even known the cup was there. To her, the cup was not even on the table because she was so focused on producing. Tina's need to produce, however, didn't come from a desire to impress her parents or prove herself. She was solely self-driven. She truly wanted to help others as much as possible, and she would forget to take care of herself in the process.

When we ignore our bodies, we slip into misalignment with our Soul. Self-care snaps us back in place, and for Tina, that meant realizing that she wanted to coach physicians exclusively on how to avoid burnout.

For both women, we incorporated a grounding practice as well.

Grounding or earthing refers to direct skin contact with the surface of the Earth, such as with bare feet or hands, or with various grounding systems. Proponents feel walking barefoot on the Earth enhances health and provides feelings of well-being. Study findings show connecting the body to the Earth enables free electrons from the Earth's surface to spread over and into the body, where they can have antioxidant effects. It also appears to improve sleep, normalize the day–night cortisol rhythm, reduce pain, reduce stress, shift the autonomic nervous system from sympathetic toward parasympathetic activation, increase heart rate variability, speed wound healing, and reduce blood viscosity.[3]

You don't have to do anything difficult while grounding (on grass, sand, concrete, touching a tree). If you like to scroll TikTok or Instagram in the morning, go stand in the grass in your bare feet while you do it. It helps you feel instantly relaxed. Some people say it's bullshit, but I say, what's the harm in trying?

---

3   James L Oschman, Gaétan Chevalier, and Richard Brown, "The Effects of Grounding (Earthing) on Inflammation, the Immune Response, Wound Healing, and Prevention and Treatment of Chronic "Inflammatory and Autoimmune Diseases," *Journal of Inflammation Research* 8, (2015), https://www.ncbi.nlm.nih.gov/pmc/articles/PMC4378297/.

If you don't have an outdoor space to stand in, there are a number of grounding mats you can check out online. Place the mat on the floor under your desk, plug it into the grounding hole of an outlet, plop your bare feet on it, and voilà: you're grounding.

PROFESSIONAL STEPS

There are personal boundaries, professional boundaries, and internal boundaries. Most of the time, if you take a look at who is steamrolling your boundaries, you'll find it's *you*. Many women relinquish their own boundaries without anyone else forcing them to.

You need to believe you have the right to your boundaries: for example, eight hours of sleep. You deserve to have your basic needs met. Every time you drop your boundaries, you invite physical deterioration into your life.

You don't have to respond immediately to every text, email, or phone call. These are boundaries that we need to hold, not only to train other people how to treat us, but for us to value ourselves. Most of us aren't even valuing our own time. We're overscheduling, and if we unload something, we immediately fill it with something else.

With Tina and Jane, I had them list out the areas where they had no protected space or time. For you, it could be with your kids. Are they sleeping with you at night? Are they barging in when you're trying to work? It could be your phone. Are you leaving it on your nightstand every night so it wakes you up when it buzzes? Are you compulsively checking it so you don't miss an email?

Look at the residual effects your lack of boundaries are having. Then, start taking steps to put your boundaries in place and honor them. Having firm limits on access to you will show the people in your life that your time is valuable and, therefore, not to be taken advantage of or wasted.

TINA AND JANE TODAY

Today, Tina is still a neonatologist but also a physician burnout coach who now incorporates self-care into her life. She could never have coached people on burnout, the original reason she came to me about, without doing some self-care and some self-examination on where her own energy was going.

To make time, she pulled back on writing so many dissertations and removed herself from some of the internal boards she sat on at her hospital. Instead of doing work that didn't feel productive, she streamlined her efforts to focus on the tasks she felt most spiritually connected to: helping sick babies and coaching physicians.

She did decide to put a pin in being a Chief Wellness Officer—with plans to work on it down the road—because she has three young children she wants to spend time with. Today she has a much deeper wellspring of energy, because the things she's focused on have a purpose and help achieve her long-term goals.

Tina proves that it's okay if you want to do a lot—as long as it isn't coming at the cost of your physical health. The biggest game changer for her was getting more sleep. I cannot stress enough the importance of sleep—it is the foundational building block of self-care. Google it and be inundated with stats on why it should be your priority.

Jane's priorities are also very different now than they were before.

She asked for more help at her job, and after opening the center, she left the company and is now working for another treatment center. She created an addiction workbook with one of her colleagues and founded a startup to help people with anxiety while flying.

She's taken a sharp turn away from what she used to prioritize, which was working herself to the bone. She's now thoughtful about what she allows into her life because she knows anything that drains her mental health will also drain her physical health. Grace is still with her, reminding her to focus on herself; however, Grace is not currently a threat to her health.

Most people can only see in hindsight the learning opportunity behind a negative experience. What's amazing about Jane is that she saw the learning *while she was in it*. She was able to be grateful and see the lesson immediately following her diagnosis. It would be hard to argue that her acceptance didn't help expedite her healing.

EXPLORE FOR YOURSELF: PLUG THE DRAINS

Pick a part of your body that you're currently unhappy with. For the next twenty-one days, exclusively send that body part positive energy, acceptance, and love.

I'm not very good at it, but some experts swear by doing "mirror work." It involves standing naked in front of a mirror and changing the narrative that's going through your head about that "displeasing" part. Give the part a name. If you hate your thighs because they're not the size of a twelve-year-old boy's, you can name each thigh: Harriet and Lucy.

I prefer to consciously glance down at my thighs, typically when I'm driving and they "spread," and send them love and gratitude. I tell myself, "I know that these are actually strong. These thighs made it okay for me to gain weight when I was pregnant so I could still easily walk around and carry a baby. They help me run and jump and do all of the things that if they weren't this large and strong with this much muscle, I wouldn't be able to do."

When you try it, it's going to feel uncomfortable. It may feel inauthentic to send this body part love and appreciation when you don't even like it. But, remember, what's the harm? There's no downside to it. And, even if those thighs never get smaller—even if they get bigger—no matter what exercise you do or what eating plan you adopt, you're still going to love them because they are you and you are them.

Start with, "I appreciate you because you are part of me, and I know that I am good and that I deserve love." If you have arthritis, when you're sitting and looking at that joint that hurts, say, "Thank you, because I know that you are an alarm saying something isn't right." When a fire alarm goes off, it's awful to hear. It hurts your ears and you just want to turn it off. However, that fire alarm is going to prompt action and bring the firemen who are then going to save you and put out the fire.

I try to think of that any time a part of my body is hurting. Instead of hating it and wishing it away, I ask, "What are you trying to tell me?"

Talking to your body in a different way will have real-life results of healing, even if it's just your mental health. Sending negative energy to it, being annoyed with it, or hating on it multiple times a day is poisoning the well of your mind.

Invite a little bit of good chaos into your life—chaos that fills your cup. For example, getting an extra hour of sleep could feel chaotic. In fact, it could feel very uncomfortable. However, if that nurtures your body, then the chaos is worth it.

If you aren't sure where your cup's level is at, practice this Fills and Drains exercise.

Envision your energy as an old-timey water tower. First, make a list of all of the things in your life that feel like a drain. They could be a pinhole leak, or they could be a giant gusher. A pinhole leak could be *I feel like shit because I didn't finish that project today*, while a gusher could be *My husband has cancer* or *My kid is autistic*. Those are all energy and emotional drains.

After you list out all of your drains, identify those that can be plugged. The shame of not completing a work task is a drain that you could plug. Your kid being autistic is not something that you can easily plug. (Please know that I'm not saying you don't love your kid if they're autistic. I'm saying it takes a lot of your energy to keep them happy, safe, and feeling loved. That's not good or bad. It just is.)

Once you look at how many drains you have and which ones you can plug, then you need to find out what the fills are. What is filling your water tower?

There needs to be enough going in to maintain a level of energy that will offset your drains. Examples of fills are: going on a walk in nature barefoot, or making yourself a delicious, healthy meal that honors your body's needs. Creative outlets are always a fill. You could play the piano, paint, write, or take photographs. I have one client who fills her tower by shopping at thrift stores. Another fill is anything that helps you physically, such as more sleep. (I know, I'm a dog with a bone on the sleep thing.)

(A note here: exercise does count as a fill, but only when practiced in moderation. If it feels compulsive, like your worth will decrease if you don't do it, then it's a drain. However, if you feel like you want to do the occasional Peloton ride because it's fun and brings you joy, then it counts as a fill.)

The Fills and Drains exercise can help you physically see which drains are always going to be there and how much time you need to dedicate to offset those drains so your tower never runs empty.

WHAT'S THE HARM?

What's the harm in believing you are worth one more hour of sleep?

BELIEVE IT TO SEE IT

DRINK YOUR OWN KOOL-AID TO MANIFEST IT ALL

"It's humiliating. I dread going out every day."

—KATE

"I'm going to show them. I'm going to be an industry titan."

—ERIN

MEET KATE AND ERIN

Kate was my very first client. She joined our first Zoom session, smiling and radiating a beautiful bright light with great energy—but I could tell she was masking something that was dimming that light.

That something turned out to be door-to-door window sales. She was cold-call door knocking to sell *windows*. Kate lives in the middle-of-fucking-nowhere, Wisconsin. It gets dark at four o'clock in the winter. It is bitterly cold. And she was knocking on doors, with a goal to knock on six doors a day.

Before door-to-door sales, she worked at a local college in the grant writing division. She loved writing but hated her job. Unfortunately, she got fed up with the job, and before she planned her next step, she threw deuces and bounced out of there. Then, a couple months after being unemployed, she started to panic.

Kate was married and had a young daughter, so she was getting some pressure from her husband to make money. It wasn't a doomsday scenario, but they definitely needed additional income. Somebody somewhere along her journey said, "Well, why don't you just go sell these windows, and you'll get a commission." It's true the commission was good; however, anybody who's ever done door-to-door sales knows that it can be humiliating. And disempowering. And above all, it's fucking hard.

Every morning, Kate woke up paralyzed with dread. Often, she wouldn't even leave the house to go knocking until one o'clock in the afternoon. She would drive around to houses, then sit in front of them, totally locked with fear. She didn't want to knock because the people who did answer the door were rarely friendly. In fact, they were almost always annoyed and rude. It was a one-in-a-million chance of finding somebody who was actually kind and bought anything from her. Plus, the job was a hundred percent commission, so most days she was working for nothing.

She was circling the drain, if you will. However, in our second session, she confided in me that her heart's desire was to be an actress and a model. While she's beautiful and bright with great energy, my first thought was, *You live in the middle of nowhere, and you're in your mid-forties. Even if you were in LA, this is no easy gig.* When you talk about a dream, this was a *dream*—and a tough one at that.

We'll come back to Kate in a sec.

Erin is a client who came to me while she was working in tech information security. In our first session, she explained that her boss was borderline verbally abusive to her. Like many women we've talked about in this book, she was being passed over for promotions and knew she needed to get out. Erin had a goal of being a CISO—a Chief Information Security Officer—within the next five years, but she knew that was never going to happen at this company. It wasn't necessarily because she was a woman however; there were multiple reasons.

Erin is a veteran who is very direct (by necessity). She's a badass, and she wears it on her face. Her toughness is very visible, and in her organization, that was not exactly welcomed. Women are expected to be agreeable, friendly, warm, and nice. While Erin is all of those things, you have to earn her trust before you see them, and she never quite understood why being agreeable and nurturing were valid in a professional landscape.

After a few sessions, I dug and tried to get more insight as to why this majestic, Soul-led woman had such a tough exterior. I learned that while Erin was in the army for five years, she'd withstood harsh treatment from higher-ranking officers. It took about a year working together before Erin confided in me that during her time in the military, she was sexually harassed and mentally abused.

She explained that, in her unit, in order for female privates to move up in ranking, they were forced to perform, or look the other way when sexual acts were performed, for superiors. If you didn't participate, then you wouldn't move up. And if you don't move up, you're stuck doing menial tasks, like scrubbing floors. You are the lowest person on the ladder. Erin refused to play along and was therefore not promoted—remaining a private her entire five years of service.

Some of her tasks included fixing tech for the army, and she remembered one specific story where they had her go underneath the desk to deal with an old-school hard drive. Then, while she was stuck under the table, her boss walked over and started mock-humping her from behind. Everyone was laughing, and she couldn't move until he was done. She was humiliated, and things like this were unfortunately happening on a somewhat regular basis. Eventually, she was discharged because she wouldn't comply—refusing to give in to the pressure.

This history was traumatizing. After leaving the military, Erin vowed that within ten years, she would be the highest private sector chief officer you could be, which was a CISO.

When we started working together, our goal was to get her closer to a CISO role. But first, she needed to leave her current position, because her boss was dismissing her feelings and calls for change, which triggered her back to her military days. We knew that she couldn't stay there.

GUIDING LIGHT: JACK KORNFIELD

Jack Kornfield taught me that there is no replacement for meditation. Everybody who's fighting it and looking for an alternative will never find it. (Full disclosure, the single exception is extreme sport players who have to be present in the moment or die, as they have the same focused experience as meditation.)

Jack explains that meditation is a journey. It can be scary to get to know the parts of you that you've silenced for so long. When you first start on your journey, you may not get a feeling of immediate relief and understanding that your Soul is talking to you. You may need to go through a cleansing of the things your mind wants you to hear that are not good. That ego mind can come in and start to say unkind things to you.

That's why when people start meditating, ten minutes in they think, *I don't like this. I have to stop.* I understand that feeling, but meditation is a muscle that you have to build. First you have to purge your mind of that running to-do list, and all the ways you could be spending this ten minutes differently, in order to create space. Once you do that, you can get into a wonderful, peaceful place where you can have conversations with the 75 percent of you that is nonphysical energy.

Jack Kornfield explains the belief that our Soul is a piece of us, but only 25 percent of our Soul is in us right now as physical energy. The other nonphysical 75 percent of our Soul is energy of the Universe. It is everything outside of us. This nonphysical piece of you has all of the answers to every question you could ever ask. This is the guiding force, the one that's nudging us. This is your intuition. This is the you that is project managing your life. And it only comes through in meditation.

Unfortunately, we rarely listen to it. Instead, we look for it in self-help books and material things. We're seeking it everywhere else *but* inside of us. And she—the Soul, the 75 percent—is begging you to give her a moment. It's like you're doing double Dutch, and she's just standing there waiting: "I'm going to get in. I'm going to get in. I'm going to get in." But first, you need to create space. You need to give it a beat so that she can come in and tell you everything she already knows.

She knows what's going to happen in the future. She sees it all. She's the one that has those moments of déjà vu, when you say, "Oh yeah, I already learned that lesson." "Oh, right. That happened before." She is the one there to guide you. She's a huge asset, and she's being ignored for the Real Housewives and a glass of wine because we *think* we don't have the time to sit and let her help us.

She can't do it by herself. She can't get you the things that you need and the peace of mind and the love that you are crying for every day if you don't even acknowledge that she's even there.

SPIRITUAL STEPS

Esther Hicks, author of *Ask and It Is Given*, has a great metaphor for the importance of meditation. Imagine you're a cork that wants to float on the top of water. The top of the water is the high vibrational plane where all of the manifestations are. Everything that you're asking for is up there. When we sleep at night, our cork rises and floats to the top.

Then when we wake, we stub our toe getting out of bed. That pulls the cork down a bit, but it's only a temporary submission and pops back up as we shake off our throbbing toe. Then we go downstairs and our kid is sick. This pulls the cork down a bit deeper. And then we get an angry email from our boss. Now the cork is deep underwater.

The cork is being pulled under by these everyday situations all day long. The longer you hang out on those lower vibrational planes, the more lower vibrational things you will attract into your life.

Kate was hanging out on a rock-bottom vibrational plane throughout the day, so she was attracting bad things. Her car broke down. The people who answered their doors would be complete assholes. All because her cork was so far submerged for so many parts of the day.

She started meditating both before and after she went knocking. Meditating allows you to break that negative thought pattern and let your cork rise to the surface. Even if you can get your cork to rise to the surface for just two to three minutes a day, you're going to be able to access some of that wonderful stuff that you want.

Meditation is the most impactful way to get your cork to rise, but it's not the only way. Another way is dancing for fun. A lot of people think it's silly, but even if you're just in your car, put on music you love, sing out loud, and wiggle your butt in your seat as you're driving. It's a huge vibrational lift.

Another way is doing something for others. When I'm having a really shit day, I go to Starbucks, order four different coffees, and deliver one to each of my friends. It immediately floats my cork all the way to the top.

Tapping into your creative outlet is an excellent way to raise your cork. You don't have to be good at it. You can paint, knit, write, or even color in a coloring book. Do something that feels totally unproductive but good to your Soul. That means you're in alignment and your cork is on the surface.

It's important to note it's not about doing more things. I could have told Kate to just work harder and become a better salesperson—that it was far-fetched for her to be an actor or a model. Or told Erin to just suck it up and deal with the abuse. However, there was *no fucking way* we were going that route. They would have never been happy.

If you are on a low vibe plane—maybe you're in a bad relationship, a job that doesn't appreciate you, or in a community that doesn't feel like a fit with your ideologies anymore—use meditations and other outlets to raise your cork. Then the Universe will send you the bread crumbs to follow to pull you totally out of your situation.

Your Soul is trying to talk to you, but you'll never be able to hear it if you don't get quiet. It can't come through when you have earbuds in all day. It can't come through when you are running yourself ragged over a to-do list. The only way your Soul can talk to you is if you create the space for it.

PROFESSIONAL STEPS

Both women needed an exit strategy because there was no viable option for them to salvage their current roles. Both Kate and Erin identified a D-Day—this was the day, come hell or high water, whether they had another job lined up or not, they were going to quit.

Just having a date in your head can provide immediate relief because you know there is an end in sight and your suffering will stop. Often people won't give themselves a hard deadline to quit because of the financial aspect. I won't lie, that's a very real fear that both women had to overcome. Erin was a single mother living with significant medical bills. Kate's family was surviving paycheck to paycheck. Yet both committed to getting out because they knew that it would motivate them to find a new job quicker and that once they picked their date, they could start to mourn.

No matter how much you hate your job, the day you leave is going to feel sad. There will still be good memories you have about working there (or you would never have joined in the first place). Most of the time, it's loving colleagues. Even Kate, who worked door to door, had to mourn. She had a great boss and she loved interacting with people, even if they were strangers.

They both told the Universe, "This is not good enough for me anymore. I deserve better." Just that act of declaration can bring you peace. When you're at peace, your Soul rises to a higher vibrational plane where you can start accessing the new amazing things the Universe is lining up for you. It may not happen the second you decide to quit (though I have seen that happen). It can take weeks or even months. But if you speak to successful people, they'll always tell you that you have to take risks.

This was a risk for both women, but they cut the tether to the low vibes and the hits their self-confidence was taking on a daily basis.

This can be powerful in relationships as well. If you're in a relationship with someone who isn't abusive, but you don't feel that connection or you're not feeling energized by the relationship, it can be good to have a mental D-Day. You can share with them or keep it to yourself, but have a date in mind that you know if something doesn't change, you're out. I know many women who have done this with their marriages. They have a date in mind, and they can build a plan around that date so they feel supported when it does happen versus withering on the vine every day.

Good things can't find you if you're in a terrible situation that's keeping you on a lower vibration. You have to rise to access all the great things in your vortex.

KATE AND ERIN TODAY

Currently, Kate has a new writing job that she loves, and she's doing modeling and acting on the side. She also got a divorce, and she told me it was the best thing she's ever done.

Once you move into a higher vibrational plane, people and things that don't match that vibe will either rise to meet you or they'll fall away. For her, it was her marriage. Walking away wasn't easy—she had to move in with her parents at one point. Yet, throughout this whole time, Kate had the best attitude. She claims meditation was a huge piece of staying positive. She knew everything was going to be okay because her Spirit was telling her it was going to work out. And her Spirit was able to get that message through because she was creating space through meditation.

Through our time together, Erin had what I can only call a spiritual awakening. She realized that she could control how her life was written. No one else was going to make decisions for her anymore. She would leave nothing up to chance. No one else could define her abilities or limitations.

Once she changed her mindset, she had four job interviews within six weeks—all for CISO positions, which was a stretch for her. Her current role was a senior director, so to go from that to a chief level was a big deal.

Erin landed the CISO job and added $150,000 to her comp. We still work together today, focusing on how she can encourage her team members to expand professionally and personally, as well as how to show some of their personal depth at work. In the past she was all business, but today, she's more trusting—a compassionate advocate and leader to her team. It's been a beautiful transformation.

Erin's mantra was: *I believe in myself, I know I can do this, and I'm going to show those who abused me.* In reality, who knows if they ever found out. This was all for her, and it was important for her to believe that she could do it. That was something she never let go of. She always believed that she could get there. However, she got there much faster once she accepted what was going on in her reality. Then, once she tapped into her spiritual center, she manifested almost immediately.

You have to believe you're worthy before you can manifest anything. Everything around you is a product of what you believe you deserve. Erin always believed she could get to that job title and she was focused on it. To her, that was unshakable. The belief was always there, but most people don't feel that way. The average person is not as determined as Erin.

We women tend to underestimate ourselves, and we underestimate the joy, relationships, and success we can have in this lifetime. When we do that, we succumb to mediocrity. We settle for less than what we want for our lives. If you're living the life that you want, and you have some desire for maybe someday getting a bigger house, that's one thing. However, if you have a burning desire to experience something in your life and you've told yourself that there's no way it's ever gonna manifest for you, that's a problem.

That's the person I'm talking to in this chapter. The person who had a business idea and then watched somebody else go do it. How many times have we looked at the shelf at a store and said, "Oh my God, why didn't I think of that?" Lots of women swear they could have created Spanx, but they didn't. They didn't because there was something inside them that never believed that they actually could.

All great thought leaders say that they had unwavering belief. It didn't matter how long it would take or in what form it came—it was going to happen.

That's why we have to commit to thinking big and not backing down.

Thinking big determines how much you can accomplish, and if you are only looking at things for the next week or the next year—getting through things versus thriving within—there are two very different realities that you will manifest.

Remember the scene from *Forrest Gump* where Lieutenant Dan is on the top of the boat during the storm? He didn't care about the storm. His attitude said, "Throw whatever you got at me, I'm staying up here. You're not gonna shake me from this place." Erin had that mindset: Throw whatever you want at me. I'm not going away, and there's no way that I'm not going to achieve this goal.

That's what the Universe does. It tests your perseverance. You can manifest anything, but it's about more than saying it out loud or making a vision board. It is having an *unshakable* determination and belief that no matter what, you're going to get it. You're going to have to overcome quite a bit of resistance and push back. Who knows how long it may take, but the Universe will always reward you.

EXPLORE FOR YOURSELF: GIVE YOUR SOUL THE MIC

You just have to do it. Put an alarm on your phone, put it in your calendar, or vocalize it to your family. You can even just do it on the weekends. Tell your family, "Saturday and Sunday from three to four, I'm going to meditate."

If you won't hold yourself accountable, use your kids. Kids are wonderful at holding you accountable. Ask your child: "Can you help me remember every Saturday after lunch to go meditate?" They will be *gleeful* to remind you. Then give them some sort of nonfood item reward for helping you.

If you don't have someone to hold you accountable, there are other options. Start a chart where you put stickers for the days that you meditated. Use an app like Streak to track your progress. Journal on the days that you meditate so you can have something to look back and see how it made you feel. How did that day go versus the day you didn't meditate? Was there a difference at all?

The important thing is that you make the connection between meditation and creation. Look for the moments where you feel more at peace during your day. For instance, you just had a terrible call with your boss. Maybe a week ago you would have carried the shame or anxiety for three days, but this time you only took a day to be unhappy about it and then let it go. Getting over tough emotions quicker is a connection you can make. Maybe you have more patience with your kids on days that you meditate.

Have an awareness of what you are handling differently. You may not feel the need to honk at the driver who was texting and missed the green light. Once you connect the dots back to why you feel more calm and have more patience, you'll gain momentum and start meditating more. You'll also find ways to meditate throughout your day. If someone is running late to a meeting, you can use that as an opportunity to sit in stillness for ten minutes instead of getting frustrated.

If something comes up while meditating that you have to remember—such as *don't forget to put this book in my kid's backpack tonight*—keep a notepad next to you while meditating. Thoughts like that can derail you, especially when you first start out. Pause your meditation, write it down, and then go back. You don't have to restart.

Your brain is like a toddler who's had too much sugar and needs to burn it off. Your mind will think of all the random crap that you were supposed to do three years ago and never did. Those thoughts don't matter. Your brain is just purging. Eventually, you'll get to the point where you don't have anything to write.

Anybody who says meditation doesn't work is full of shit. Period. They're not trying.

Side note: be prepared to have some physical reactions. When I first started meditating every day, I got sick. I got a really nasty cold that took a while to move through my body. It was a cleansing. My friend Rachel got pneumonia for three months. Just know that if you do get sick afterward, it shouldn't be an association that meditation isn't working. It should show you that it *is* working. Your body is clearing out all of the negative vibrations so you can start with a clean slate.

You can also connect your mindset to milestones. Think back over your life. Highlight different milestones in your life—both the low points and high points. Try to remember your mindset when each milestone happened. There's a correlation between your mindset and the event. Then, truly believe that it was how you were feeling or thinking that created that reality.

Going forward, try to be in your Soul as much as possible. Your Soul is divinely worthy. When you look back at some of those events and you can take accountability for the manifest power that you had, even in the hard times, it deepens your belief that you can manifest positive things for the future.

For example, let's look at a negative relationship. I've dated some bad dudes in the past, but one in particular was borderline cruel and an alcoholic. Now I can look back on that and see that because I did not love myself at that point in my life, I absolutely attracted him to me. I believed that I was only worthy of a not-so-nice guy, so I manifested him. Now I can look back on the relationship and take ownership: yep, I manifested that. BOOM. Took my power back.

Again, I feel the need to make one thing very clear though. If you were abused as a child, you did NOT manifest that. I'm talking about events that happened when you were an adult or at least old enough to have a self-awareness of your thoughts and your feelings. Go back to those times. It's easy to look at the good things you manifested: a job, a move, a wonderful person who came into your life. However, it's important that we also review how we manifested the obstacles in our lives too.

Once you can take credit for it all, good and bad, that's when you're really unstoppable. Then, when you start to have goals or desires, it's easy to believe that you can manifest them. After all, you manifest everything. Everything in your life is a direct correlation to what you believe you deserve. Take a look around. If you believe you deserve to be more physically healthy, then that journey will be easy. If you are struggling on your health journey, chances are you're probably not fully believing that you deserve to look however you wanna look. A lot of us would love to look like Giselle, but how many of us believe that's meant for us?

WHAT'S THE HARM?

What's the harm in listening to what your Spirit is trying to tell you?

GRATITUDE IS A VERB

RAISE YOUR VIBE SO HIGH THAT
ONLY GOOD STUFF CAN FIND YOU

"I hate my job. Everybody talks down to me. I feel invisible."

—SUSAN

"Feeling depressed, lost, and losing self-worth when my passion and hard work at home and in the office is undervalued."

—KERRI

MEET SUSAN AND KERRI

Susan has a story that's unfortunately common among women in their early fifties. They have a wealth of experience but are starting to be overlooked for promotions. People assume that they're starting to wind down their career rather than aggressively pursue the next opportunity within their organization.

Susan was an incredible human resources expert who had all of these big ideas for the Fortune 500 company she worked at. She was constantly going above and beyond her job description, and then, you guessed it, they hired somebody younger to come in and be her boss.

This event triggered her to reach out and start our work together. She didn't like the trajectory of her career. She felt that her company was trying to keep her in a holding pattern until she retired, even though she was much more qualified than the person they had her report to.

When people get overlooked, they get resentful, which breeds a lot of anger—and Susan was *very* pissed off. This soft-spoken, beautiful woman was trying to keep the lid on her anger in our sessions, but I could see and feel her emotions brewing under the surface. "Can you fucking believe these people?" was the vibe she radiated. However, this was at the beginning of 2019 and the job market was tough. It was a hiring manager market, not supportive of candidates. She was afraid to leave her job where she'd been for eleven years, and she wasn't sure she could start somewhere else because of her age.

She also felt behind on her knowledge about current technology, which gave her company an excuse to not give her the same opportunities that younger new hires were getting. Then she said that they were starting to say that her attitude wasn't great.

Imagine this. You're feeling pushed out. You're more experienced than the person they just hired above you—and then they're telling you that your attitude sucks. Susan was starting to fall prey to the situation many women in the last quarter of their career experience: that her company was setting the environment to piss her off, to make her feel unvalued and dismissed, to send the message to be quiet or go away. She was starting to walk into their trap because she was very angry, even though she wasn't an angry person by nature.

Her parents were first-generation immigrants, and she had done everything an immigrant was supposed to do. Her husband owned his own business. They weren't crazy rich, but they were comfortable. She had invested in her education. She had climbed the ladder. She had been quiet when people didn't want to hear her. She had walked the line, and now they were forcing her into the exit lane of her career highway. It didn't feel fair…because it wasn't fair.

More on Susan in a minute.

Kerri is another client who was being pushed down and pushed out of her twenty-five-year job in insurance. One of the "reasons" she was put on a PIP (performance improvement plan) was because she was too "assertive" and "blunt." Not exactly actionable items. Nevertheless, this criticism left her more than a bit insecure.

Kerri wanted me to help her soften her approach. However, I didn't see being assertive as a problem; the problem was the organization she was trying to confine to. If that was how they were going to treat her after twenty-five years, it was time to read between the lines. They weren't trying to get her to change her personality—which is ridiculous to begin with—they were trying to push her out without a concrete reason.

Kerri had been categorized as a "lifer," and the company wanted fresh blood with a new perspective. In my mind, if you stay anywhere past five to seven years, your stay can become a liability versus an asset. Once you stay at a company too long, people begin to look at you differently, as if you're coasting or comfortable or unable to "cut it" somewhere else.

While they wanted her to change her communication style, what I needed Kerri to see was that her communication was her superpower. She just needed to find a company that recognized it as an asset versus a liability.

As we began working together, I asked her if the situation was salvageable. We agreed it wasn't. They had hurt and embarrassed her with their baseless claims and performance plan. However, Kerri was scared to leave the cage. The Universe wasn't having it and made the conditions even worse. The company started doing weekly humiliations. On a national call, they announced a new role for her, which was a demotion, before it was ever cleared or communicated to her.

She was full of resistance, and she was becoming a fraction of the amazing, powerful, confident woman she was at heart. She was worried that leaving the company would ruin her reputation in the insurance industry. The final straw was when the company came to her and told her that while they had told her she could work remotely from Indianapolis, they had changed their mind and she had thirty days to move back to Pennsylvania.

Kerri was a military wife. She couldn't just up and leave the base her husband was stationed to. She finally listened to the message the Universe was sending her and believed it was time to step out of her cage.

GUIDING LIGHT: DEEPAK CHOPRA

"Be happy for no reason like a child. If you're happy for a reason, you're in trouble, because that reason can be taken from you."

—DEEPAK CHOPRA

Deepak tells us that it's okay to have desires. In fact, we're meant to have desires for the things we want to manifest in our lives. However, we have to be careful what the intention of our manifestation is. If we're asking for something to please our ego, our happiness is going to be really short lived. We all know this feeling. We buy the stuff, we open the Amazon box, and we get a little dopamine hit. But then it fades.

The more we keep trying to buy our happiness, the more it's going to have the opposite effect. We're going to feel more and more empty because we're going to be disappointed that the purchase didn't fix it. The gratitude and the fulfillment that we want to feel on a daily basis *has* to come from within.

Once you are in a place where you are okay not getting what you want is when you get it. When you need nothing is when you get everything. It's okay to have desires for physical manifestations and material things. We're meant to do that. However, when we start using that as a replacement for things that can bring us deep, personal, spiritual joy and fulfillment is when we start to get in trouble.

When what you're manifesting does come, it may not come in the way you thought. Say you want to go to Italy and shop at all the designer boutiques. Is it because you want the stuff or is it because you want to experience another culture?

The Universe might not give you that trip to Italy and the money to shop at all those places. What it will do is bring somebody from Italy into your life that you could learn from. You can get that cultural fulfillment from people who are in your own community.

We have to look at our desires and understand that once you can be grateful for everything you have, the good and the bad, the Universe will send us the things we want—and by then, you're probably not going to want or need them.

SPIRITUAL STEPS

Susan (and Kerri to a lesser extent) also started gratitude exercises. Susan especially needed to love the job she had in order to attract her next opportunity. This was the biggest, hardest obstacle for her to get over through our time together: feeling gratitude for a job that she went to every day and dreaded. She had reached the point where she hated going into the office.

Susan started a new routine that she followed every day before entering the office. She would sit in her car in the parking garage, and before she got out, she would say, out loud, three things she was grateful for about her job that day. It could be that it was paying her bills, that it was putting food on the table for her children, or that it allowed her to use the experience and knowledge that she got through her education. Then, every day before she walked through the threshold, she would say three times, "Thank you. Thank you. Thank you." Please note though that gratitude guilt can also shush the voice of your Soul that's begging you to level up. Susan did not use gratitude as a place to hide or as a way of overriding her Soul's wishes for a better job. What we did was feel gratitude for what she had while also noting that she deserved better and was excited for the "better" to manifest.

We focused on raising her vibe so high that her boss would either have to match it or fall away, by talking about what wonderful qualities she could identify in her. Her boss was new and therefore could possibly help Susan see things from a different perspective. At the time, Susan didn't love the perspective this woman had, but it didn't mean that she had nothing of value to offer or that they couldn't work together.

Susan was now going into her office every day with a much different energy. She was vibrating at a much higher level. She would anchor herself in this place of gratitude. After a few weeks, the difference was incredible. On our calls, we would talk about the job opportunities that were appearing, and she'd say, "They're okay, but I'm not unhappy anymore." Nothing had really changed at her job, but Susan's perspective completely changed.

Now, we weren't trying to get Susan to a place of acceptance for a job that was not up to her standards or to accept a mildly abusive work environment. It was about getting Susan to see the blessings and the gifts that she had in front of her, because that was the portal to getting something better.

Once you start looking at things that you dislike through a lens of gratitude, it changes your whole life. Susan's anger was totally gone. The fights that she would have with her husband every now and then, because she was annoyed and grumpy when she came home from work, stopped happening. Sure, shit happened during the day that annoyed her, but she managed her energy and her vibrational level throughout the day so much that the negativity didn't come home with her anymore.

She also no longer woke up and dreaded the drive to work. In fact, for her drive, she started listening to specific podcasts to help her get into the right headspace for the day. She had a thirty-minute commute each way, which was a perfect amount of time. This was now her carved-out time. She was not allowed to think about work or the negative aspects of her job while driving. Imagine entering an environment or a situation from a positive headspace: it changes everything.

Kerri also practiced gratitude, especially for her thirty-day deadline. She practiced self-care and gratitude for the time the company gave her. She viewed it as a gift, which changed her whole energy from shame to anger to gratitude and acceptance. She used the month as paid exploration time for herself. As her energy changed, her vibes raised and she manifested a new position.

PROFESSIONAL STEPS

Both women needed to understand their value. We started by creating a list of personal "wins." This could be anything from surviving an abusive relationship to growing up in poverty. Maybe your parents got divorced. That can cause kids deep trauma, and to be able to live through that and become a thriving adult is a big deal. Don't miss the opportunity to claim the strength of enduring life events. However, it can also be *I didn't lose my shit at my kid two mornings ago when they wanted to tie their own shoes when we were already late.*

Then, every day, I had them add one thing they accomplished to the list. It could be I got up and washed my face even though I didn't have any Zooms today. I worked for three hours without scrolling or checking my phone. I went for a twenty-minute walk. I meditated for ten minutes. I made my kid a healthy breakfast. The key is to get the ball rolling.

Acknowledging your "wins" is critical because people can try to tear you down, whether in a professional or personal relationship. Sometimes it can come from inside you. This can bury all the good things about you. But by reviewing your list and adding to it daily, you prime your brain with all the amazing things you have already done. It's not an affirmation; it's a fact about yourself.

Add to your list every night before you go to bed. Make sure to write down at least one thing, but if you can add fifteen things, even better. This doesn't have to be something you're grateful for, just wins for that day.

On the professional side, you should start keeping a love file. Anytime your boss sends you an email saying you did a good job, screenshot it, save it as a PDF or JPEG, and add it to your file. Anytime a client writes you something nice or tells you they're satisfied, add it to the file. Any thank-you cards, compliments from coworkers, nice comments on your LinkedIn posts, save. These are all tangible reminders you can review when your brain is in a hole. Or if your company starts trying to push you out or create invalid reasons to fire or demote you, you have a file filled with counterpoints that prove you've done a great job.

You can also ask the people in your life what they think you're good at. While external validation shouldn't matter to you, it can bring to light things about yourself that you never realized before.

SUSAN AND KERRI TODAY

About nine months into our work together, Susan accepted a job offer from a company much closer to home. It was a promotion from the title that she had at her original job. While Susan didn't see drastic career changes overnight—she didn't have multiple offers within three weeks, like some of my other clients—she also wasn't suffering at the level that she was when we first started.

She took back control over her emotions and her feelings, and how she was going to spend her days. Susan was someone who immediately grasped, and then utilized, the gratitude exercises. She could have stayed at her job for those nine months and been fucking miserable. I guarantee that her relationships would have deteriorated, and she probably wouldn't have interviewed as well as she did. In fact, she probably would have been stuck there and then accepted a lousy early retirement package.

Susan had let these external circumstances come in and dim her light. She was removed from the bright, positive energy that is her Soul. Her story is a wonderful example of changing the energy with which you meet your circumstances if you can't immediately change the circumstances themselves.

It's also a testament to not letting people push an agenda for your career that you're not ready for.

During her free month, Kerri interviewed and found an incredible new job that loves and appreciates her. It's a breath of fresh air. They pay for her to travel when needed and put her up at the nicest hotels. She says she feels like she's in a whole new realm of existence. She feels free.

EXPLORE FOR YOURSELF: RAISE THE VIBE UP IN THIS BITCH

If you are in the so-called "older" age bracket, I see you. I see what they are doing to you and it is not okay. You do not have an expiration date. Work as long as you want. Your value doesn't diminish as you age—it only grows.

Advocate for yourself to your employer; stand up to them. If they don't see your value anymore, you absolutely have options. You can leave and find something else. Women can get caught in their own head thinking that it's going to be hard for them to find something else or there's just going to be way too much ageism so it's never going to happen. If you feel that way, then that's going to be your reality. However, the truth is that you can play to your strengths. Your age is an asset, not a detriment. That's where you win. Look at industries and categories that value your vast experience and tenure.

In your current position, identify the things that are a thorn in your side, big or small, that bother you or that you try to avoid because it feels like there's some negativity tied with them. Instead, make a conscious effort to proactively send those things or those people love.

You don't even have to be in the same room as them. A lot of times before I do a meditation or before I go to bed at night, I will think of somebody to send love to. It's kind of like saying prayers but instead, you're saying prayers for other people. You can send love to things you don't like, but you should also consciously send love and good vibes to the people in your life who are a support or who you're grateful for. Try to draw in more blessings to their lives like that.

You can also write out five people that you're just grateful for. Then another five that you aren't grateful for. Maybe you have a shitty landlord. Maybe your boss is not being great. Maybe it's a family member that you feel is really shady with you. Take time daily to send all of those people, good and bad, love and good vibes. Say out loud what you hope for them (good things only). Then see how things shift and how their response to you will shift.

Once you stop focusing on what you want for yourself, and you start focusing on being grateful for other people and trying to manifest things for them, amazing things start coming to you too. But manifestation happens right when you don't care about it anymore. When you're focused on somebody else, stuff will start to flow to you with ease.

Now, gratitude doesn't happen all the time. I'm not saying that I float around on a cloud, all day every day. You're going to get your feathers ruffled, but the more you can go back to that place of gratitude, the less suffering you're going to have. It's a decision. Some days you just feel like wallowing in the negativity and that's okay, too. It's going to happen. Eventually, though, it's important to pull yourself back to a place of gratitude and get back on a higher vibrational plane.

If you're struggling with gratitude, find an accountability partner and text them every single morning for seven days, three things you love about your job or boss—no repeats. This can be hard. I had both Susan and Kerri do this with me. You can send things such as *They want the company to be successful* or *They gave me the opportunity to come into this job, which has given me financial security*. It can be as simple as *This person is really funny* or *This person has been an advocate for me in the past*.

You can always find three things that are good about a person or job. Focusing on the good changes your energy. You're not going to come to a call with an aggressive attitude if you've just texted three things you appreciate about your coworker.

WHAT'S THE HARM?

What's the harm in spreading love and gratitude?

A LESSON IN HUMILITY

ESCAPING CAREER CONFINEMENT

Don't we all have a treasure trove of external judgment? People think that they're protecting you by showing "concern," but they're not. They don't get that giving you opinions that *they* think are helpful is really resistance. They're really making it so much harder for you to follow your path.

For me, this topic has certain family members written all over it. I got a lot of grief when I moved to Chicago with no plans of ever going back to St. Louis.

Junior year of college, I was offered an internship with glacéau (maker of **vitamin**water)—but in Boston, not St. Louis. Great, sign me up. I showed up in Boston with two suitcases and no place to live. I went to see some places for rent, and they weren't great. My mom ended up finding a long-lost cousin who happened to live in Cambridge proper. I spent a summer living with this guy who turned out to be a damn psycho, but it was worth it because not only did **vitamin**water have a job waiting for me when I graduated, but living in a major city opened my eyes to a whole new world.

The day after graduating from Mizzou (University of Missouri), I packed up my white 2001 Nissan Altima and drove to Chicago. Once again, I didn't have a place to live but I did have a job and coworkers who were incredibly supportive resources. The Universe was looking out for me, because the day I arrived, I was able to find an apartment with a neighbor, Angie, who took me under her wing and provided comfort on the days I felt overwhelmed.

Now, I had just graduated from the prestigious University of Missouri-Columbia J-School, which is one of the best journalism schools in the country. When I moved to Chicago, some of my family could not understand why I left, because no one ever had before. To be a good Midwestern daughter, you had to stay close to your family and be dutiful.

My job was entry level and not glamorous. Days were spent filling up 7-Eleven shelves, or dragging around a cooler full of **vitamin**water and smartwater, cold-calling on convenience store managers in my branded polo shirt.

One day, I was on my knees, filling up a cooler, freezing my tail off, and I thought, *Are you friggin' kidding me? I have a degree! I'm better than this.* I got impatient and quit, even though I loved my **vitamin**water family and co-founder Mike Repole, who was an incredible role model and who, unbeknownst to me, had a long-term plan for my career.

I went to work at Robert Half International, a huge global recruiting firm, solely because they had an office on Michigan Avenue and I got a $15k bump in pay. I got to wear a suit and had a fancy title: Head of Communications and Marketing for the Chicago office. I was that elegant person waiting on the El platform in my H&M suit with my Starbucks, going to my job in a high-rise.

And I was fucking miserable.

Every single day, I left work and cried. I had no freedom. I was chained to a desk. There was a petty receptionist who would call my boss in Colorado and tell her if I was even five minutes late. They even monitored how many minutes I took for lunch. It was awful.

After ninety days, the director of that division, who was a gigantic prick, called me into his office and told me that I was fired with no severance. He gave me a box to pack up my desk and had security walk me out. I couldn't believe that people could be treated like this. **vitamin**water would never do something like that. They wouldn't just throw people away. Humiliated, I left with my box of stuff, and my then boyfriend, now husband, came and picked me up. I sobbed the whole way home.

I immediately called my old boss, and I begged for my job back. I confessed I had made a huge mistake. I took the "high-rise job" because I thought it *looked* better. Even though I thought it impressed my friends and my parents, the reality was that it was awful. My boss checked with Mike who gave him the green light to take me back, but I'd been demoted and had to reprove myself and my loyalty to the company.

I swallowed my pride. I took the job and got my very valuable company equity shares back. (When I started, I had stock, and when I left, I obviously forfeited those, but I did fight to get my stock back.) From there, I worked my way up to being Director of National Accounts.

I had changed jobs for *other* people. I did it because I thought I was better than a job in sales and I wanted other people to see it as well. It didn't matter that **vitamin**water felt like a family and that I had freedom to take a two-hour lunch if I needed it. It didn't matter that I had built trust with them. I gave all of that up to wear a suit and tell people that I worked on Michigan Avenue. That was a real eye-opener, and I'm glad it happened. I never took another job again based on the name on the door or how much I thought I could humblebrag to my friends.

Instead, I made the choice to work for companies with leaders like Mike. Those were the best experiences and where I made the most money. I wanted to work for people who trusted me and were going to give me personal freedoms. I broke free from the prison of doing things because of how it would make me look or because of what people would think.

I built a life in Chicago even though I always felt my family never fully understood or accepted it. I learned I had to stop caring what other people thought. Zero fucks mentality. I did what was right for me and my family, and I've always been greatly rewarded for that.

When you tell people you're going to leave your multi-six-figure-a-year job to go be a coach, everybody has an opinion on that too. Certain family members didn't, may still not, understand that decision either, but I did it anyway. It's not that you don't stop, think, and take into consideration when people give you genuine advice. You have to embrace zero fucks and say, "I just don't care what you think. I'm going to do what I feel is right for me, regardless of your opinion or *concern*."

GUIDING LIGHT: RYAN

After I'd made the decision to walk away from my career, my husband, Ryan, never let me entertain the idea of working for anyone else ever again. On the days I panicked and started looking for a "regular job," he was the person who reminded me that I'd burned the boats.

After a few terrible job interviews, he was a strong but gentle reminder that if I worked for anyone else again, I would never forgive myself, and that our girls were on Team Mom. They are watching me follow my Soul, and if I went back to the old way of working, I would not only be betraying myself, I would be a hypocrite to our children.

And he did this with love. Just like when I work with people and can see things they can't, he could see what was best for me. He knew that it was going to be okay. He was my personal cheerleader, constantly pumping me up.

I worry sometimes that we're living the Liz Show, and I tell him, "What's your Purpose? I don't want to leave you out of this." And every single time, he looks at me and says, "My Purpose is to support you. You are the light I want to be around."

When someone believes in you with such depth and passion, you can't go back. You have to burn the boats (which you'll learn about in the last chapter). Ryan would pull me through the resistance muck to the other side, reminding me of the vision I had for myself on the good days. At every low point, he reminded me that highs were on the horizon.

Find your person who can be there for you. It can be a loving spouse or partner, a sister, or best friend. It just needs to be someone who wants to see you soar. No part of them can feel competitive with you or have an ulterior intention for you. Someone who wants you to run free, to play in the lush abundance that's on the other side of your fear. If you don't have someone in your personal life, find a coach. An amazing coach is not going to let you go back into the cage.

FORGIVE YOURSELF

HOW TO TAKE THE MEGAPHONE
AWAY FROM YOUR INNER CRITIC

"I have moments when I feel like a total failure and that consumes me."

—MEGAN

"I'm a 'fixer' for everyone else…but myself."

—GWEN

MEET MEGAN AND GWEN

Megan was a fifteen-year veteran of a large athletic company that is known to be—how do I put this?—cultlike. The culture there is toxically loyal. People don't ever leave. If you get there, you stay there.

Megan's dad was a famous distance runner who won two New York City Marathons, was a two-time runner-up in the Boston Marathon, and was renowned for running 110 to 150 miles per week to train for road racing.

He was quoted as saying, "Somewhere, someone in the world is training when you are not. When you race him, he will win."

With that in her blood, it's no surprise that Megan followed suit and became an ultramarathoner. She ran from LA to Las Vegas in seven days *by herself.* She's a cut-from-a-different-cloth kind of person. When we first started working together, I could sense that she never cut herself any slack and had ultrahigh standards, which spilled over into her personal and work life.

I assumed that because she was so passionate about the sport of running and also longed to feel like part of something great, she withstood not-so-great treatment from her employer. During her time working for this larger-than-life athletic apparel company, she was laid off *twice.* To make it sting even more, after each layoff, they would come back and hire her on a contract basis to do product launches for less money.

In our first session she explained how she was unemployed and living on her friend's couch in Portland because she couldn't afford a place by herself anymore. This woman had lived and breathed that company for fifteen years. Now that they had laid her off again, she had hit rock bottom.

Her mindset was extremely self-defeating. She constantly thought nothing she did could ever be good enough. Maybe it was the downside of having a father who was a superstar.

She was so committed to the company that she even had their logo tattooed on her finger. The company was very much a "This is your family now" kind of place, and when that family rejects you several times, it can destroy your psyche.

On a few of our coaching calls, Megan would hold back tears. It was heartbreaking to see such an incredible woman, athlete, friend, and creative genius feeling so unhappy and so stuck that she couldn't see her way out of it.

Megan's consulting rate was extremely low for the work she was producing. We agreed she needed to raise her rate. I told her she had to increase it at least 50 percent and charge a program rate instead of an hourly rate. She was running huge product launches and was the sole go-between for the brand and celebrities. She wasn't a PA or helping out on a set; she was the connection to huge athletes, DJs, and influencers.

When she told the company her new rate, they countered even lower than what they had paid her on the last project! It was a giant middle finger. She finally had enough.

The day after she said "I'm done working for them" out loud to herself and to me, she got an offer from everyone's favorite global athleisure brand—her top-choice role and employer. But the only way that job could have manifested to her was if she cut that cord and broke free. She moved the moped.

One of the things she wanted to manifest was being able to run on the beach. In Portland, she was running ten to twenty miles or more—basically a marathon—in cold, rain, and mud every night. Think about the mental strength and commitment you have to have to run that much every single day. Her former employer was taking advantage of these traits, because she was driven, committed, and loyal. It was almost as if the worse they treated Megan, the more she wanted to prove them wrong and win them over.

So many women fall into this trap. They're afraid to leave their "good" job because the outside world is telling them they'd be crazy to leave. It's the same with relationships. There are women who are unhappy in their relationships, but they think, "Well, he doesn't hit me. He has a job. He's a decent father. I'd be dumb to leave." It doesn't fucking matter. It's all relative. If it's not good enough for *you*, then you should leave.

Gwen is a communications expert who worked on political campaigns for five years. Unfortunately, the overwhelming stress led to an alcohol addiction. One fateful night, she got a DUI, and because she was a semi-public figure, she had to endure a very public shaming.

Afterward, she left politics and moved back to her home state of Oklahoma, where she had grown up on a cattle ranch, and married a farmer who had three little girls from a previous marriage. Gwen is tough as nails and has been since childhood.

In our first session, she explained she felt like she was hiding and living in shame from her DUI. Almost as if to punish herself, she was doing zero self-care. She explained that it wasn't even worth trying because she had too many demands on her time combined with extremely high (self-imposed) expectations—she'd fail at any practice she attempted. We concluded that she had been distracting herself for fear that if she slowed down even a little bit, she'd hear those voices that were constantly judging and nitpicking her apart—and it would have taken her under.

Gwen was waking up at 6 am., going straight to her desk, and checking emails. She'd only work until five p.m. on the nights she had the girls, but without the kids there, she'd work late into the night—and this was during a pandemic. Prior to being confined to her home, she'd been traveling constantly. She took a deep dive into a work addiction, unable to recognize that she was working herself to death hoping to overcome the shame of her past.

Any spare time she managed to find, she put toward the new house they were building, obsessing over every little detail. She didn't think she could count on anyone else. However, the real reason that she couldn't delegate any of her work was because she needed it to boost her self-esteem. She had very competent team members working under her, and they were saying, "Hey, give me some of this. I'll take it off your plate." But she couldn't because deep down she thought it might question her self-worth.

GUIDING LIGHT: TARA BRACH

"Staying occupied is a socially sanctioned way of remaining distant from our pain."

—TARA BRACH

Tara Brach teaches self-acceptance. She preaches that we shouldn't postpone feeling happy with ourselves until whatever it is that we've placed around the corner has come to fruition. When we start comparing ourselves to other people, not only do we demotivate ourselves and invite negativity in, but we rob ourselves of any joy in the moment. If we can be here right now, void of comparison, then we will see the accomplishment, the beauty, and the joy as it exists in the present moment.

We screw ourselves when we try to hold out or deny ourselves acceptance and joy because we think it will help us get to our goal faster. It actually moves the goalposts farther away on all the things that we want. If we do manage to get there, we're still not going to be happy. By accepting ourselves right now, as we are, we can experience the joy of this moment while still working toward your goals.

SPIRITUAL STEPS

I had both Megan and Gwen take the human design quiz.

Human design is your energetic makeup. It's like taking a professional assessment for your energy and the Purpose of your life. Think of it as the spiritual version of the Myers-Briggs test.

There are five main types. To find out which one you are, you take the human design quiz, which takes five minutes. You include your birthday, time, and location, and you get your results, which help you see what you're here to do.

I'm a Projector; my job in this life is not to work. I'm not necessarily supposed to be producing things. I'm supposed to have the big ideas and then put them out to people. I'm supposed to talk about them, mention them, and then wait for the doers, the Generators, to come into my life and bring them into reality. I learned that I need time to energetically build up my reserves. This gave me permission to have four-day workweeks, taking Fridays for myself. I learned I have to take that break to purge energies from coaching sessions and realign so I can be better at what I do. Doing less helps me do better.

I'm telling you, this test gives you another level of self-awareness.

Human design is like the contract your Soul makes with the Universe about who you came to be and what you came to do. You manifested in this physical form under the agreement that you were going to be whatever you are. When you understand your blueprint—and you can take or leave certain pieces that don't feel right—then you can communicate how and what you need to work with other people.

It gives some context as to why you may like doing some stuff or why you don't. If you like doing certain stuff, you're in alignment with your vortex. If you don't, you're out of the vortex.

A lot of people beat themselves up because they don't have insights into what kind of person they are. It can be applied to your career and how you interact with coworkers and bosses, and to your personal life and how you interact with family and friends. Once you understand how you work best, you can communicate this to the people around you. You don't have to tell your boss you're a Projector. You can say, "I have figured out that I need a little bit more time on projects because if I take more frequent breaks, I'll have more insights and the finished product will be mistake free. You'll get higher-quality content from me than if I work with this deadline."

There's no downside to taking it. What do you have to lose?

PROFESSIONAL STEPS

Both women started writing morning pages. Originally created by Julia Cameron, morning pages are similar to pages of gratitude with a twist. First thing in the morning, you write out three pages, front and back, of whatever is in your brain. No censoring, no spell checking, no judgment.

It's a great way to silence the shame megaphone and transport yourself into things you are excited about, things you feel grateful for, and things that come to you when you're in the creative flow. This is a tactical way to create more distance between the thoughts of judgment and shame, and set yourself up for a great day.

It really doesn't matter what you write down. If you have to, write "I don't know what to write" over and over again for three whole pages. There's no wrong way to do morning pages. Other things to write about are your current worries, what you dreamed about, your grocery list, affirmations, how your coffee tastes, what the weather is doing, etc.

Your morning pages are you-time. Don't give up this time for your family or work (remember our conversation about boundaries?). Everything else in your life can wait. This is your time to clear your thoughts. Purge everything that distracts you during the day.

There are only two rules: write three pages and don't let anyone else read them. You don't even need to read your own writing back. If someone else reads your writing, you'll be less likely to be honest, and you'll lose all the benefits that morning pages bring.

MEGAN AND GWEN TODAY

Megan moved to LA, is thriving in her new job, and has a ton of friends. She continues to train for various races, but now she's running on the beach rather than in mud.

Gwen got less focused on the day-to-day tasks at work and more focused on the larger strategic things that she wanted for her career. She started off-loading tasks to her team members. She realized that having to do all the work herself was making her look less competent. When people hold onto work and they don't delegate it, it makes them look like an insecure leader.

She started walking more, and she helped her husband around the farm. While she was out in nature, helping with the harvest, she started thinking of new ways that they could utilize the farm. She started considering running for city council to try to increase tourism and then work with other farmers so that they could cross-promote events. She got healthier and lost some of the weight that she felt was unnecessary.

Gwen is a big thinker, but when you're living in a prison of your own judgment, it's hard to take risks. For her, failure would equal shame, which would drag her back into a place of humiliation and self-doubt. By doing the deep personal work, she freed herself from her prison and thrived.

EXPLORE FOR YOURSELF: GET TO TAPPIN'

Retrain your conscious and subconscious mind with affirmations and EFT tapping.

Before you start using affirmations, it's imperative to acknowledge that the things that you're currently telling yourself are lies. No amount of shit-talking yourself will ever be motivating—at least not in a healthy way. You being hard on yourself is not the healthy way to grow or to achieve whatever goal it is. It's doing 100 percent the opposite. It's why you aren't doing better at work, and it's why you aren't attracting the partner you want. Even hiring managers can feel it. If you're not loving on yourself, why the hell should they?

Start by taking a hard look in the mirror and acknowledging when you're saying something that is hurtful, and that the 75 percent nonphysical you is not on board with it. If it's not something she would say, then it's not something you should say.

Then, you can get some affirmations going. There's a wonderful app called I Am. You can set it to go off as many times a day as you want. It has wonderful affirmations such as: I am strong. I am resilient. I am worthy of abundance.

You just have to start telling yourself new lies. I say lies because they're going to feel like lies in the beginning. It's going to feel like, *No, but I'm not beautiful. I'm not incredibly strong. I'm not a genius.* The thing is, you're already lying to yourself with the judgments you're putting on yourself. So, why not replace those lies with good ones, empowering ones? At some point they won't feel like lies, once you say them enough. You'll start to believe them, and you'll start to see the truth in them.

EFT is another powerful tool to rewire your subconscious mind—some have even dubbed it psychological acupressure. The emotional freedom technique (EFT), sometimes also referred to as tapping, is an alternative to the traditional treatment for healing pain and emotional distress. It uses your fingertips to stimulate energy points in the body. Gary Craig, the creator of EFT, reveals that the treatment sprung from the idea that the cause of all negative emotions is a disruption in the body's energy system.

EFT works by tapping on the supposed paths through which "life energy" is believed to flow in the body (meridian points) to release blockages. These specific pathways of energy help balance energy flow to maintain your health. Imbalance of energy flow can result in a laundry list of negative feelings.

A 2019 study[4] involving 203 individuals tested the physical reactions and psychological symptoms of people attending EFT workshops—the majority being women. Participants reported experiencing significant reductions in anxiety, depression, and PTSD symptoms, as well as in pain levels and cravings. They also reported improvements in happiness. Physical measures in a subset of participants showed improvements in heart rate, blood pressure, and levels of the stress hormone cortisol. Other research[5] found that students with anxiety reported that EFT helped them feel calmer and more relaxed.

Here's how to give it a try:

1. Concentrate on the negative emotion—fear or anxiety, a bad memory, an unresolved problem, or anything that's disturbing you.
2. Establish a setup phrase that describes the current issue you are facing. The three main goals you need to focus on are:
   A. Recognizing the issues
   B. Accepting yourself despite the problems
      i. For example: "Although I have this (fear or problem), I deeply and completely accept myself." You can alter it according to a way that suits you.

---

4   Donna Bach et al., "Clinical EFT (Emotional Freedom Techniques) Improves Multiple Physiological Markers of Health," *Journal of Evidence-based Integrative Medicine* 24 (February 2019), https://www.ncbi.nlm.nih.gov/pmc/articles/PMC6381429/.

5   Elizabeth Boath et al., "Tapping Your Way to Success: Using Emotional Freedom Techniques (EFT) to Reduce Anxiety and Improve Communication Skills in Social Work Students," *Social Work Education* 36, no. 6 (2017), https://doi.org/10.1080/02615479.2017.1297394.

    c. Refraining from addressing another person's issues as your own

       i. For example, you can't say, "Although my boss is an ass-hole, I deeply and completely accept myself." Instead, you can alter the sentence by saying, "Although I'm sad that my boss is critical of me, I deeply and completely accept myself."

3. While maintaining your focus, use your fingertips to tap five to seven times each on nine of the body's meridian points:

    A. Top of the head: directly in the center of the top of the head

    B. Beginning of the eyebrow: the beginning of the brow, just above and to the side of the nose

    C. Side of the eye: on the bone at the outside corner of the eye

    D. Under the eye: on the bone under the eye, approximately one inch below the pupil

    E. Under the nose: the point between the nose and upper lip

    F. Chin point: halfway between the underside of the lower lip and the bottom of the chin

    G. Beginning of the collarbone: the point where the breast-bone (sternum), collarbone, and first rib intersect

    H. Under the arm: at the side of the body, approximately four inches below the armpit (bra line)

4. Tap on these meridian points while aiming to accept and resolve the negative emotion, which will help repair any energy disruption.

Tapping sends signals directly to the stress centers of the brain, thus reducing the anxiety or negative emotion you're experiencing. The resulting goal is for EFT to ultimately restore balance to your disrupted energy.

WHAT'S THE HARM?

What's the harm in telling yourself a new lie?

BURN THE BOATS

HOW TO ESCAPE FROM THE MUNDANE

"I was bedridden for three months. My husband had to shower me and help me on and off the toilet."

—BETH

MEET BETH

Hopefully by this point in the book, you've started to look at your life and begun evaluating whether or not it feels good enough. Are you going to be okay living at your current level for the rest of your life with zero fear or regret?

Beth is a wonderful example of a client who took a look at what she was doing on a daily basis, the contribution she was making, and decided it wasn't good enough. However, she had some major obstacles to overcome before making changes. Beth first started working with me to gain a work–life balance, as well as to overcome some chronic, physical pain issues, which she had already acknowledged were due to her stress load.

She had a thriving Etsy and Amazon store that made custom calligraphy birth announcements, wedding invitations, etc. She had built it into a six-figure business, grossing about $150,000 a year. While she had two seasonal part-time helpers because the holidays were always a huge time for her, she was doing all of the printing, shipping, designs, and day-to-day tasks herself.

When Beth came to me, she was uninspired, exhausted, and restless. She knew that she had plateaued with her business and needed to either double down on it to get revenue to $300,000 a year (to cover costs and make it worth her time) or walk away from it entirely.

On our first call, I asked how she had reached this point in her life, and she explained that not only was the business at a plateau, but she had also started to feel symptoms of her Guillain-Barré syndrome (GBS) coming back.

If you're unfamiliar, Guillain-Barré is a completely debilitating chronic illness that affects your nervous system. This disease had put her in the hospital for three months, only two years prior to our call. During that time, she was bedridden, completely reliant on her nurses and family to wash, go to the bathroom, eat, and literally anything she wanted to do. She had three young children, all under the age of ten at the time.

Can you even imagine being a high-performing mom-preneur and at the same time battling to even sit up or walk? Through a lot of physical therapy and diet changes, she managed to leave the hospital, but for a long time, she still needed her husband to help her with everything. It was a very, very long road to recovery, and Beth lived in fear of it coming back. Guillain-Barré isn't something doctors are quick to announce that you're healed from as it can often flare up again down the road.

In our sessions, Beth explained she was cruising toward burnout. She wanted to avoid that *and* she wanted to avoid GBS coming back.

GUIDING LIGHT: MICHAEL BERNARD BECKWITH

Michael Beckwith is the Founder and Spiritual Director of the Agape International Spiritual Center, a transdenominational community headquartered in Los Angeles. Highly regarded for his teachings on the science of inner transformation, Dr. Beckwith embraces a practical approach to spirituality utilizing meditation, affirmative prayer, and Life Visioning™, a process he originated.

At first glance he may look like a preacher, but I find him to be more of a spiritual enthusiast who helps everybody by emphasizing connection and acceptance. Oprah has said, "Michael teaches that the vision we set for our lives begins a sacred process of unfolding that unlocks everything that is unique, mighty and magnificent inside each of us." So, in a nutshell, he checks out.

His books have helped not only me, but my clients, get to a place of higher consciousness, where one can visualize exactly how they want their life to be. His book *Life Visioning* explains the four stages of spiritual growth and consciousness.

Phase one is **Victim Consciousness**. You're still blaming other people for everything and saying the world isn't fair. When you're in this state, you're asking questions like:

- Who can I blame?
- Why me?
- Why is this so hard?
- What's wrong with me?

The way to transcend that and move to the next stage is to start asking different questions:

- What's my Purpose?
- What would you have me do?
- How can I be of service?

Then you have to get to a place where you can find stillness to receive the answers because, as he says, the Universe will always answer.

Once you start asking these questions and begin receiving answers, you can move to phase two: **Manifest Your Consciousness**. You start understanding why you manifest specific things in your life.

In the previous stage, you're in the victim consciousness thinking, *This job sucks; why can't I find anything else?* Then you start to realize that you've got unlimited potential and that you're a divine being—you're not here to do some job that feels hard or draining eight to twelve hours a day. Then you start getting psyched and excited, thinking, *Okay, well I can manifest things.* It's time to get specific around setting intentions for the life you want to manifest. This is when you start creating vision boards and focus wheels, and dedicating time to experience the feelings that will come once you have them.

The next phase is a bit controversial—at least among self-help gurus. Wayne Dyer believes you shouldn't talk to anyone about what you want to manifest. Instead, wait for your manifestations to show up first, because if you invite any low vibrational energy or negativity into that very fragile place, it can get squashed. However, I tend to side with Michael Beckwith, believing that you should talk about what you want to do, but *only* with a limited pool of people who have proven they unconditionally support you. These are people who will be excited for you. These are people who will check in and hold you accountable for your progress. This is a great time to get a coach or join a supportive program where everybody's trying to grow together.

This is NOT the time to share it with people who will give resistance or the "well-meaning" family and friends who are concerned about what you're doing—frenemies who in the past have swooped in with a bunch of "concern" and stomped all over your little manifestation seedling trying to grow.

I had a lot of people who were concerned when I walked away from my career. They said, "Are you sure this is the right time? I mean you have a lot on your plate already: a two- and four-year-old, a new city. Maybe just try it out as a side hustle before going all in." But not only did I predict their responses, I immediately shut them down and explained that feedback like that was not welcome and definitely not supportive.

Instead of letting that low vibe penetrate, start writing down goals: weekly, monthly, annual, and five-year goals. There is magic when you write down your plan and put it in a place where you can see it every day.

Then, you have to give up the resistance that will come around all of this. Anytime we're trying to grow, we know that it's going to trigger resistance. You just have to keep moving forward.

Michael has a great quote that I love: "Pain pushes until the vision pulls. The pain is trying to force you into having a vision that's greater than the pain. Potential is always bigger than the problem you're having." This quote is genius. It means you just have to keep focusing on what's on the other side and knowing that it's going to all be worth it.

Phase three is to **Become a Channel**. Becoming a channel means you have to vibrate at the level where all of the things you want are. When getting pregnant, I would argue you have to be in a mental state to allow that miracle into your life, even if it wasn't planned. You may not have known you were in that state, but you were probably at a high vibrational level when that baby was conceived so you were in alignment with all of these wonderful external circumstances to manifest that.

It's the same when you're trying to "birth" this new life. You have to find the space to believe that it's going to come, just like having a baby. You don't even see your baby for the first term (it's the size of a watermelon seed), but you believe it's in there. You tell yourself, "I know something's in there. I'm confident that it will come to fruition and will be this wonderful thing that I've always wanted."

When creating your new life, you have to have faith that just by you living, breathing, and believing in it, it's already manifesting all of the work. The behind the scenes is taking care of itself.

When you're a channel, you start to ask, "Show me the signs."

Phase four is **Being Consciousness**. This is the top of the mountain. This is when you hold true to the knowing and belief that you are a piece of God. Once you realize that there can be no disconnection, then you know that everything that you desire for yourself, if it's meant for your higher good, will manifest.

You need to be clear on what you want, yes, but you also need to understand these levels and the journey that you will go on, so that you can see the ultimate end result, which is having the highest level of consciousness. Every thought you have, every move you make, and everybody you interact with are all a part of this bigger picture. You are unstoppable both on a conscious and physical level.

And if this is good enough for Oprah, isn't it good enough for us, ladies? Oprah didn't get where she is by not buying into this stuff.

SPIRITUAL STEPS

"What's my next step?" A question you've no doubt asked yourself before. Most of the professional steps in this book map out a clear, tactical thing you can do. But for your spiritual side, it's about getting into alignment so everything you want can manifest. A great way to get alignment is to do things that bring you joy. (I know, obvious, right?)

If you like painting, paint—even if you are terrible at it—and have zero expectations for how it will turn out. And you're not allowed to hide it or throw it out if you don't like it for at least one year.

One of my Guiding Lights assigned me this task and I was immediately resistant. So, you're telling me I have to spend money on art supplies, carve out time to sit and paint, and clean up the resulting mess? For what? The very high probability that I'll have an ugly painting that will be a reminder of that failure for a full year?

Yep. Ever the diligent student, I overcame my doubts, bought all the stuff, and painted a rather large 3.5-foot landscape painting. After it dried, I hung it as the prominent centerpiece of my office (you can see it if you watch some of my old YouTube videos). While I was not impressed with my work, as the year went on, it started growing on me. I began to see the beauty in it. I accepted it for what it was: a creative outlet that didn't want to be dissected and judged. I'm happy to report that I haven't thrown out the painting; instead it hangs in my bedroom and is often the first thing I see when I wake. It's a wonderful reminder to give myself grace each day—there is beauty in whatever will unfold, if I choose to accept it.

Unfortunately, a lot of women don't know what brings them joy. If that's you, it's time to perform a joy audit. Look back at your habit tracker. What items on there put a smile on your face and make you excited? That feeling of excitement is a great indicator that you are on the path to joy.

If your day is filled with things that don't bring you joy, it's time to change what you're doing. Don't go to a job that is soul sucking. There is no amount of soul sucking that you should be able to handle.

I hear you saying, "Well, what brings me joy doesn't pay the bills." Today, you can make money doing anything. However, it may take some time to get there. Don't expect to get monetary gains immediately on this journey. That can actually suck the joy out of the experience. But don't save your joy project just for the weekend, either. If you enjoy doing it, engage in that joy as often as possible because feeling that joy benefits you in so many ways.

You'll wake up with a sense of purpose. Your relationships will improve. You'll look forward to every day. Engage in your joy every day, even if it's just for thirty minutes a day.

PROFESSIONAL STEPS

Beth knew what her Soul was telling her to do, but in order to commit to an internal vision, you have to create an external vision that other people can see: personal branding. You have to be your own hype woman, your own publicist. A lot of people think you have to have your own business or be an entrepreneur in order to have a website, to be a guest on a podcast, or to write articles. In my humble opinion, that's just not true.

The more visible you are, the better. Write articles and post them on LinkedIn, Medium, or other websites. Create profiles for yourself on podcast booking websites such as Podbooker. It's free to create a profile, and when you're listed as an available guest, podcasters who are looking for guests with a specific subject matter expertise can find and book you. It doesn't matter what industry you are in—there's a podcast for it.

SOCIAL MEDIA

Social media use has become so mainstream that not having a social media presence is deemed suspect—especially by recruiters. When an employer looks at a résumé, they're only getting a basic overview of who you are professionally, so your social media helps them fill in the gaps and get a deeper sense of who you really are.

Over three-quarters of hiring professionals believe that checking a candidate's or employee's social media profile is an acceptable way to vet them. Make sure that your personal social media profiles are private, because if not, they have the potential for serious repercussions in your professional life. In a 2020 survey by the Harris Poll[6], 70 percent of the employers who responded said they believe every company should screen candidates' social media profiles during the hiring process. Moreover, 78 percent of employers believe that current employees should maintain a work-appropriate social media profile.

Recruiters want to know who you are. Your ability to mesh well in a potential employer's company culture carries a lot of weight. Now more than ever, companies are focused on understanding who a person is and what their values are.

Now that you understand that not having a curated social media presence can affect your bank account, it's time to create a public professional Instagram account. I get that you likely don't want to dive deeper into the soul-sucking abyss that is social media, but you don't have to. You can find people on Fiverr to manage it by creating content and posting it for you; aim for at least one LinkedIn post a month and biweekly Instagram posts.

Not only will having this added account help your SEO (search

---

6   Sheena Karami, "71% Of Hiring Decision-Makers Agree Social Media Is Effective for Screening Applicants," PRWeb, October 14, 2020, https://www.prweb.com/releases/71_of_hiring_decision_makers_agree_social_media_is_effective_for_screening_applicants/prweb17467312.htm.

engine optimization), but it's a way to curate what recruiters and hiring managers see. Things like entertaining clients, attending industry events, and doing things you enjoy that are self-care related, such as cooking, walking your dog, or home organization.

Things to avoid posting: anything violent, profane, explicit, or illegal. Also save the bikini and drinking pics for your private personal account.

BETH TODAY

First, Beth leaned into leveraging her past pain into a future business coaching the loved ones of Guillain-Barré sufferers. Second, she leaned into her calligraphy company. She hired two additional full-time workers who were, essentially, able to run that business without her. With delegation, she was able to spend way more time with her kids and be at home with them even during their holiday rush season.

Once the Etsy store started cranking, Beth started writing a Guillain-Barré syndrome blog, which developed into her wanting to coach those affected. She wanted to take this awful experience, own it, and then help people on their journey, because she and her husband had no one other than doctors to turn to for advice when she was at her lowest. There was a great white space for her to make her own.

Within two months of leaning in to the coaching, she had five clients. Throughout her journey, she grew and became more confident. At the time of our last session, she told me she was going to put a pin in everything and go to medical school.

She wanted to take her coaching a step further, and to do that, she needed medical training. She wanted to become the physician that could tell patients there was hope, and her medical advice would be supplemented with the holistic and spiritual actions that helped her. She wanted to be the doctor who told patients they didn't have to live with the pain forever.

She was willing to move her family for this dream. After her two years of school, they would have to move for her residency, because there were no options in their small town. Her husband was on board. The kids were on board. The people who weren't on board were her extended family—her parents and her partner's parents thought she was nuts and that this was totally unnecessary. Why couldn't she just keep doing the print business and the coaching? They thought she had a full plate as it was.

I want to be clear that I never had the idea that she should become a doctor. She showed up and declared it out of the blue. This is what happens when you turn on the faucet of messages from your Soul: it will urge you to level up.

Beth burned her boats. She shut down her printing business, which had generated a net revenue of at least $150,000 annually. She shut down her coaching business and quit a day job she'd started at a local university. With three kids, they needed her income—so this was a massive act of faith. It's *so* hard for people to burn the boats when there's money involved; I get it. It's very easy to walk away from something when you're not making money at it. The real test is when you're making six-plus figures and still decide to walk away to follow a bigger dream.

Now, I'm not necessarily saying that this is going to be everybody's path or that it can be everybody's path. Everyone has very real financial obligations, and you have to keep that in mind. However, the Universe will rise to meet you when you decide that you're going to walk a different path and you commit to it. The support that you need will come. The opportunities to make money from new and creative ways will come. The most important part is taking decisive action versus having your feet in two different boats. Indecisiveness is going to take you out of the game.

EXPLORE FOR YOURSELF: RUN FREE

Every time you want to turn and run back to your comfort zone, ask yourself: "What's the alternative?"

What's the potential for future regret? If the potential is anything over zero, then you have to keep going. Knowingly walking away from something you know you'll regret abandoning is unacceptable.

It's time to step out of the cage and into the lush garden waiting for you.

WHAT'S THE HARM?

What's the harm in mapping out a better life?

CONCLUSION

It's time to wipe away the fog from the mirror so you can see that you are divinely perfect just as you are, right now, in this moment.

You have everything you need already living inside you. You don't need to go out and buy anything; it's all there. It's always been there. You need to be able to trust in the unseen players that are begging to get your attention and help you look. Supportive people are waiting on the bench, and it's time to start calling them into the game. Every day that you're not utilizing them, you're not living to the fullest. Those days add up to years, and the years add up to your life.

I know this book is asking a lot of you. It's asking you to trust yourself, and to trust in something you can't physically hold—something that most people want to disprove or be skeptical of. But if you're reading this book, you know that something is missing.

At the end of the day, you have to make a choice. You can keep doing what you're doing, or you can create a new path. But really, what's the alternative to not using the practices provided in this book? That's what I always ask my clients: what's the alternative of not trying to address your relationship head-on, of not trying to get a new job, of not feeling spiritually bankrupt your whole life?

The alternative is always some form of suffering.

If you want to keep suffering, keep doing what you're doing. If you don't, if you've just invested hours reading this book, what's the harm in doing at least some of these things? What's the harm in having a spiritual awakening and adding five to six figures to your comp?

Know, though, that every step of the way there will be resistance. Sometimes the resistance will feel like it's going to take you out, but it's like a wave at the beach. You have to dive under to get through. This is not gonna be easy. Any book, coach, or person that says it's easy to have a spiritual awakening and transform your life is lying. It is, however, always worth it.

IT'S TIME TO GET STARTED

Pick one chapter and focus on that. Whether it's with one of my clients or with me, find a point of similarity in one of these chapters—whichever one you had the most fun reading or felt the most seen in—and do the practices in that chapter. Start there. If you get shaky or need some more help, download my app, *Coach Elizabeth* or visit elizabethpearson.com to get tons of free content, and I'll be the voice in your head helping you through it.

YOU ARE NOT ALONE

I hope by reading this book you feel like you're not alone in anything. Not only do you have the ability to get everything you've ever wanted out of life, but there's a whole stadium of guides and angels and nonphysical beings who are there waving the green flag. They're screaming to you, "Go for it! We got you!" Once you trust and believe that, amazing personal and professional success will flow to you. There is no grind. There is no hustle. Instead, allow the belief to wash over you, almost like a current that can take you to all the new things and all the places you want to go.

This is the part of success that so many people don't cop to. There are a lot of uber-successful people acting like they did it themselves: that they grinded and they hustled and it just happened. The *fuck it did*. They didn't do it on their own. They did it with a team of support people both here on earth and with the help of some very, very powerful allies who aligned stuff for them in the spiritual realm.

It's time for more people to come out of the "spiritual closet." We need a community—a movement of people who are willing to openly talk about the role spirituality played in their success. If we can all get on board, there can be a formative domino effect of how we treat people at work, what we prioritize in company cultures, and how we live our lives.

If you believe in this, talk about it. Keeping others in the dark and pretending you got what you wanted solely through sheer force of will is keeping everybody else who's unhappy feeling like they're just not good enough, strong enough, or smart enough to get it.

People don't give credit where credit is due, and it makes us all feel bad about ourselves. It's like these women who are walking around out here with Botox and fake lips, and then they're not acknowledging the surgeon who made them. It's fine that you got these things, but let's talk about it. Let's be real about it. So many of these billionaires aren't copping to the fact that they use astrologers, mediums, and the guidance of their Spiritual Board of Advisors. There's no TED Talks where they're giving credit to Spirit—not to be confused with organized religious figures (which bugs me, if you couldn't tell).

Collectively, if we can overcome our skeptical brains, and acknowledge that all human beings are spiritual creatures, magic can unfold. At the end of the day, if we're spiritual creatures, if we're energy and atoms and quantum physics, then there's only an upside to trying everything we talk about in this book.

I can't wait to see what you accomplish.

ACKNOWLEDGMENTS

I want to thank:

MY HUSBAND

Ryan, you have been in the book-writing trenches with me the entire time, and this would have never manifested without you refusing to let me bail on this dream. All of the support and extra-long hugs you forced upon me paid off. You remain the best decision I ever made.

MY GRANDMAS

I inherited your no-bullshit attitude and it's served me, and my clients, well. I take comfort in knowing that I can talk to you whenever I need you. Even though you're not on this physical plane, you guide me more than you were ever able to while you walked this earth. Thank you for the sacrifices you made to give me this wonderful life and immense privilege and opportunity.

MY BABIES

Delilah, you are the flower child of love and bright energy that lights my life. Your notes on my office whiteboard helped get me through this long process, and your infectious laugh rings in my ears louder than the doubts that fight for my attention. You will change the world, just like you've already changed mine.

Vivian, you are the tiger that inspired this book cover. You have a wildness that I hope is never tamed. Your relentless pursuit of fun, and risk, in any situation teaches me how to come further out of my cage. You are an unstoppable force that pushes this family forward and out of our comfort zones.

MY SISTER

Kate, your devotion to your family, your faith, and your community is a daily inspiration. How you do everything you do, while also chasing your entrepreneurial dreams, is inspiring. Thank you for always picking up when I call, texting right back, and being the compassionate ear I need when I'm "spinning."

MY PARENTS

Mom, I can only hope that I have taught my girls through words and example what you taught me—that hard work always pays off. Your commitment to philanthropy and helping those less fortunate has always been remarkable.

Dad and Vicki, I know it hasn't always been easy to embrace my life's path, but I always knew in the back of my mind that you were there and were proud of me. Whenever you said anything positive to me or taught me something, I heard it all, and it meant something.

MY EXTENDED FAMILY

The members of my extended family have always embraced me as "one of their own," and it's gone a long way toward helping me be unapologetically authentic. Thanks to Phil, Barb, Ron, Andrea, and Shawn.

MY WALL OF SUPPORT

The list of Soul Sisters who helped lift me up along this journey is long, and you know who you are, but here are a few who were there really "in the shit" with me when I needed them:

Sarton Mular-Fenton, you've always embraced me for me. Regardless if I was up or down, you've been a steady hand of support for the last twenty-two years of my life. You are a diamond in a world of cubic zirconias.

Rachel Moorhead, your friendship was the tipping point in my life that encouraged my spiritual awakenings. You took a risk inviting me to Miraval, and I'm forever grateful for that, and for your unwavering support.

Natalie Sterlin, Jessica Grizzel, Jessica Rose, and Shelly Detken, I'm grateful for your ability to help me find perspective and laugh through almost anything.

MY MENTORS

To all the individuals I have had the opportunity to be led by or watch their leadership from afar, I want to say a special "thank you" for being the inspiration and foundation for this book:

Mike Repole
Jeff Sevick
Rohan Oza
Amy Gordinier
Amy Ries
Tammy Hazen
Mari Lee
Mike Perez
Lindsay Kaplan
Amy B. Scher
Tejpal

MY BOOK-CREATION DREAM TEAM

Having an idea for a book and turning it into a book is harder than it sounds. I especially want to thank the individuals who helped make this happen. Complete thanks to Rea Frey, Anastasia Voll, Karren Kinney, Nena Madonai Oshman, Chelsea McGuckin, Skyler Gray, Joy Yeou, and Marilynn Allen.

MYSELF

In the words of Snoop Dogg: "Last but not least: I want to thank me. I want to thank me for believing in me, and for doing all this hard work. I want to thank me for never quitting."

RESOURCES

I mention a lot of tools, books, and recommendations throughout this book. Instead of you having to search for them individually, I've included links here for you to easily find what you need for your personal journey.

PODCAST RECOMMENDATIONS

- The School of Greatness
- Jess Itzer
- Mel Robbins

AMAZON STORE

- All of my favorite books and spiritual items can be found on my Amazon store for easy shopping: @Coach Elizabeth Pearson

MEDITATION

- Guided Chakra Balance on Apple Music:

https://music.apple.com/us/album/guided-chakra-balancing-meditation/341025592

- Hemi Sync Meditations on Apple Music: https://music.apple.com/us/playlist/hemi-sync-meditations/pl.u-pMyll2viX7Xxy

CHANTING

- Mantra Girl: https://www.sikhnet.com/gurbani/artist/mantra-girl (she can also be found on Apple Music, Spotify, and Amazon Music)

EFT

- "Nick Ortner's Tapping Technique to Calm Anxiety & Stress in Three Minutes": https://www.youtube.com/watch?v=02b-N4JFx10Y
- The Tapping Solution App lets you customize what you want to "tap" for (i.e., letting go of self-doubt, money mindset blocks, mom guilt, etc.): https://play.google.com/store/apps/details?id=com.datechnologies.tappingsolution&hl=en_US&gl=US

READS

- *Ask and It Is Given: Learning to Manifest Your Desires* by Esther Hicks
- *Thank & Grow Rich: A 30-Day Experiment in Shameless Gratitude and Unabashed Joy* by Pam Grout
- *E-Squared: Nine Do-It-Yourself Energy Experiments That Prove Your Thoughts Create Your Reality* by Pam Grout
- *The Teachings of Abraham Book Collection: Hardcover Boxed Set* by Esther Hicks

- *The War of Art* by Steven Pressfield
- *E3: Nine More Energy Experiments to Make Joy, Fun and Finding Miracles* by Pam Grout
- *The Power of Now: A Guide to Spiritual Enlightenment* by Eckhart Tolle
- *The Course in Miracles Experiment: A Starter Kit for Rewiring Your Mind (and Therefore the World)* by Pam Grout
- *No Death, No Fear: Comforting Wisdom for Life* by Thich Nhat Hanh
- *Going Home: Jesus and Buddha as Brothers* by Thich Nhat Hanh
- *Anger: Wisdom for Cooling the Flames* by Thich Nhat Hanh
- *No Mud, No Lotus: The Art of Transforming Suffering* by Thich Nhat Hanh
- *The Pocket Thich Nhat Hanh* by Thich Nhat Hanh
- *Bringing Home the Dharma: Awakening Right Where You Are* by Jack Kornfield
- *You'll See It When You Believe It: The Way to Your Personal Transformation* by Wayne W. Dyer
- *Living the Wisdom of the Tao: The Complete Tao Te Ching and Affirmations* by Wayne W. Dyer
- *Manifest Your Destiny: The Nine Spiritual Principles for Getting Everything You Want* by Wayne W. Dyer
- *You Are What You Think: 365 Meditations for Extraordinary Living* by Wayne W. Dyer
- *The Power of Intention: Learning to Co-Create Your World Your Way* by Wayne W. Dyer
- *10 Secrets for Success and Inner Peace* by Wayne W. Dyer
- *Change Your Thoughts - Change Your Life: Living the Wisdom of the Tao* by Wayne W. Dyer
- *Getting In the Gap: Making Conscious Contact with God Through Meditation* by Wayne W. Dyer

- *Excuses Begone!: How to Change Lifelong, Self-Defeating Thinking Habits* by Wayne W. Dyer
- *Being in Balance: 9 Principles for Creating Habits to Match Your Desires* by Wayne W. Dyer
- *The Amazing Power of Deliberate Intent: Living the Art of Allowing* by Esther Hicks
- *The 48 Laws of Power* by Robert Greene
- *The Law of Attraction: The Basics of the Teachings of Abraham* by Esther Hicks
- *Money, and the Law of Attraction: Learning to Attract Wealth, Health, and Happiness* by Esther Hicks
- *The Processes: Ask and It Is Given, Volume 2* by Esther and Jerry Hicks
- *The Vortex: Where the Law of Attraction Assembles All Cooperative Relationships* by Esther Hicks
- *Do the Work: The Official Unrepentant, Ass-Kicking, No-Kidding, Change-Your-Life Sidekick to Unfu*k Yourself* by Gary John Bishop
- *Hood Feminism: Notes from the Women That a Movement Forgot* by Mikki Kendall

SOCIAL MEDIA

- Follow me on Instagram @coach.elizabeth.pearson
- Follow me on Facebook @coachelizabethpearson77
- Connect on LinkedIn @coach-elizabeth-pearson/
- Subscribe to my YouTube channel for free video content explaining some of these tactics and ideologies: Channel Elizabeth Pearson (a great option if you are more of a visual learner).

ORACLE DECK

- My favorite oracle deck and the one I gift to all my clients: **The Spirit Messages Daily Guidance Oracle Deck: A 50-Card Deck and Guidebook** by John Holland.
- A fun animal spirit deck to use with your kids: **The Wild Unknown Animal Spirit Deck and Guidebook** by Kim Krans.
- **The Starseed Oracle** by Rebecca Campbell is for readers whose Souls miss "home."

GROUNDING/EARTHING

- *The Earthing Movie* by Josh and Rebecca Tickell is a documentary which explains the benefits of grounding/earthing.
- Amazon has many options for grounding mats which fit under your desk so you get the benefits while working inside.

LIFE VISIONING EXERCISE

- Download free PDF here for my Life Visioning worksheet https://drive.google.com/file/d/1l96JAYfkBGPo6ZfVHJc-nO8oXwQWp-GUf/view
- Totem Readings with Rachel White: Shaman, Medium, Meditation Coach. www.totemreadings.com
- *Journey of Souls: Case Studies of Life Between Lives* by Michael Newton, Ph.D.

ABOUT THE AUTHOR

You already know that **ELIZABETH PEARSON** is a renowned executive coach, but what may not be obvious is her deep love for anything "witchy": tarot readings, past life regression, crystals, runes, oracle decks, Akashic records, the works.

She's awesome at putting together IKEA furniture in record time—and enjoys it.

While she loves to meet new people, watch out—she is a self-proclaimed profanity aficionado and probably won't want to hear about your kids. She'll want to learn about YOU. She likes to go deep right away. She's allergic to small talk.

She pitched four variations of this book to "big publishers" over the course of five years and received forty-two rejections. Only when she pushed all the chips in on herself did this book become a dream realized.

Her paternal grandparents were farmers from Missouri, but not until starting her own business did she ever really understand how courageous they were and the guts they had to never work for anyone else their whole lives.

Learning more about them not only inspired her to be her own boss, but shined a light on the fact that they've been powerful protectors and aids along her entrepreneurial journey. It's taken several detours throughout her life (the subject for another book), but she's had support from her angel horde every step of the way. Those ancestors have been a massive driving force in her journey—particularly one "loudmouth New Yorker" who's up there leading the charge.

Made in the USA
Monee, IL
07 October 2023

44108902R00139